Architectural Aesthetics

BLOOMSBURY AESTHETICS

Series Editor: Derek Matravers

The Bloomsbury Aesthetics series looks at the aesthetic questions and issues raised by all major art forms. Stimulating, engaging and accessible, the series offers food for thought not only for students of aesthetics, but also for anyone with an interest in philosophy and the arts.

Titles published in the series:

Aesthetics and Literature, by David Davies

Aesthetics and Architecture, by Edward Winters

Aesthetics and Music, by Andy Hamilton

Aesthetics and Nature, by Glenn Parsons

Aesthetics and Film, by Katherine Thomson-Jones

Aesthetics and Morality, by Elisabeth Schellekens Dammann

Aesthetics of Care, by Yuriko Saito

Philosophy and Painting, by Jason Gaiger

Architectural Aesthetics, by Edward Winters

Architectural Aesthetics

Appreciating Architecture As An Art

Edward Winters

BLOOMSBURY ACADEMIC
LONDON • NEW YORK • OXFORD • NEW DELHI • SYDNEY

BLOOMSBURY ACADEMIC
Bloomsbury Publishing Plc
50 Bedford Square, London, WC1B 3DP, UK
1385 Broadway, New York, NY 10018, USA
29 Earlsfort Terrace, Dublin 2, Ireland

BLOOMSBURY, BLOOMSBURY ACADEMIC and the Diana logo
are trademarks of Bloomsbury Publishing Plc

First published in Great Britain 2023

Cover design by Louise Dugdale
Cover image: Qasr al-Farid (meaning 'Lonely Castle') at the
archaeological site of Madâin Sâlih in northern Saudi Arabia,
Ahmad Al Hasanat, Wikimedia Commons.

A catalogue record for this book is available from the British Library.

A catalog record for this book is available from the Library of Congress.

ISBN: HB: 978-1-3502-1099-8
PB: 978-1-3502-1100-1
ePDF: 978-1-3502-1101-8
eBook: 978-1-3502-1102-5

Series: Bloomsbury Aesthetics

Typeset by Integra Software Services Pvt. Ltd.

To find out more about our authors and books visit www.bloomsbury.com
and sign up for our newsletters.

This book is dedicated to the memory of Kenyan poet, Khadambi 'Nat' Asalache (1935–2006). Nat studied architecture in Nairobi and fine art in Rome. He was awarded the M.Phil in philosophy of mathematics by Birkbeck College, University of London. Although he and I were, contemporarily, graduate students in philosophy at Birkbeck, it was in the French House in Soho that we met over glasses of red wine. He was also a novelist. Khadambi Asalache, notwithstanding his eccentricities, was at home in the world. He was a very dear man.

CONTENTS

LIST OF FIGURES

PREFACE

A great many students, passing through the school of architecture at which I taught aesthetics for more than twenty years, had enormous talent. The architects who taught them in studio somehow managed to guide their talent in such a way that graduates had become excellent designers. However, I found it puzzling that neither student nor tutor had a very clear idea about what architecture is. It seemed to me, also, that their endeavours were directed towards the art of architecture – before the business of building cluttered up their lives with all the necessary professionalism and endless compromise that goes into getting a building built. Both student and tutor seemed engaged in the demands of design in a more protected and innocent way than would occur in the employment towards which their studies might head. In this book, therefore, I try to throw some light on what architecture is, by considering the attitude we take up towards its works and by discussing the nature of the medium specificity that determines its works. The strategy is to look away from buildings and to seek instead an understanding of our motivation in building, in occupying and in appreciating architectural works as an art.

ACKNOWLEDGEMENTS

I am grateful for advice and helpful comments from Anji Clark. For his critical comments and continual good humour, I thank the irrepressible Derek Matravers. I am grateful for conversations in Paris and London with John Kulvicki. There are many architects and architectural theorists with whom I have had disagreements. Demitri Porphyrios, Tanis Hinchcliffe and the late Robin Evans, in particular, I am indebted. The working out of those differences has been both enjoyable and illuminating. Students who went on to become tutors and have continued to discuss matters of architecture with me include Jo Hagan, Sarah Akibogun, Lisa Fior, Dominic Cullinan, Charmaine Lay, Nic Clear and Charlotte Skene-Catling. My thanks to the team at Bloomsbury Philosophy, who have been very patient in guiding this project through to conclusion. In particular, I am indebted to two readers solicited by Bloomsbury, whose anonymous comments have been helpful throughout. My greatest thanks are to Vanessa Perry, my wife, who studied architecture and has put up with me through the slow progress of writing this book.

Introduction

I First thoughts

It is customary to begin a book such as this, a philosophy of architecture, with a survey of historical views. In part, we shall observe this custom, though some may be disappointed with what immediately follows. This is my act of contrition; or, at least, my justification in advance. The philosophy of architecture is, as I understand it, a vein of exploration in aesthetics. That narrowly focused seam is not to be undertaken as part of the history of ideas; neither is it the history of architecture. It depends upon those two disciplines, only insofar as they have something to offer by way of giving rise to philosophical puzzles we might have in aesthetics, or as providing insights as to how we might solve such puzzles. Sometimes the theory of architecture can include all manner of detail that need not concern us, and Vitruvius' *Ten Books* provides many examples. That is not a criticism of Vitruvius. It is to warn that our aim converges upon Vitruvius' thinking, only where that which he writes upon bears on architectural aesthetics, as that is now conceived.

To look at architecture independently of its historical development is not to ignore history. We can find fruitful connections between the ancients and our own thoughts on architecture which, therefore, cross the historical divide. Thus, when we identify examples of architectural thinking in antiquity that correspond to modern or contemporary views, we grasp the commonality between the two, rather than see the one as a precursor or antecedent of the later version.

Since aesthetics, as a branch of philosophy, did not properly exist a few decades before the birth of Christ, it is hardly surprising that we find little that might be called aesthetics within Vitruvius' writing. Nevertheless, during the Renaissance, Leon Battista Alberti, a painter, architect, theorist and poet, sought to use Vitruvius' work as a template for his own discussion of architecture, *On the Art of Building in Ten Books*, first published in 1485 (Alberti 1988), some thirty-five years after he published *On Painting*.

It was not until the eighteenth century that aesthetics became a serious study of beauty in general, and of beauty in the fine arts in particular. Throughout this book we shall be looking at the illumination cast by thinkers of this period, and at the systematic development we have seen since then. Not entirely without dissent, but, nevertheless, with overwhelming agreement, the eighteenth century regarded architecture as a fine art.

II Part One: The wide conversation surrounding architecture

The book is arranged into three parts, divided variously into nine chapters. The first long chapter is spent hunting and gathering, combing the fields that surround philosophy in search of what might provide insight into the nature of architecture, and from whence it appeared. Numerous dissociated intuitions are gathered, and these form the threads of a fabric to be woven together in Parts Two and Three. It lies within our human nature to find shelter, warmth and comfort, and so the basis upon which we might set out lies *in here*, in that 'hard-wired' nature. The fine arts, by contrast, varied in their number, are *devised* by us. We do not, unthinkingly, make works of art. Ants and bees, those wonderful social creatures, often invoked to provide analogies with human endeavour, do not build nests and hives *as art*. (These six sentences might already have started an argument.) Thus, Chapter 1 attempts to get a grip on the character of just what dwelling is, *for human beings*. We shall have cause to compare our modes of dwelling with those of other creatures during the wider conversation of this chapter.

Having demonstrated both similarities and differences between animal habitats and human dwelling, we proceed to look at natural human habituation as the basis from which architecture can be seen to have emerged. What is it that grounds our conception of home, and what influence does that have on our desire to build?

In our quest, we find others, too, in search of home. Carl Jung, the psychoanalyst, is in east Africa, in search of a myth that will explain his ambivalent feeling of not quite belonging. Jung thought himself a follower of the German philosopher, Immanuel Kant, and regarded the collective unconscious, with its archetypal images, as revelatory of our pre-dispositional natures. Mythology, for Jung, is a repository of our archetypal thinking.

We find architectural theorists describing the hearth as a primordial centre, either of family or of tribal life. It is mythology that awakens us to the importance of architecture as a fundamental block in the emergence of culture. Ants and bees neither depict nor relate stories of ancestral gods and their divine shenanigans. We are pre-disposed to so do.

Chapter 2 is shorter, intended to form a bridge between part one, in which it sits, and part two; between the landscape already reviewed and the citadel of philosophy upon which we set foot in Chapter 3. In Chapter 2, we look at the discussion between Socrates and Phædrus; Augustin Aguirre's design for the School of Philosophy and Arts at University City in Madrid; the educator, poet and Nobel Laureate, Rabindranath Tagore's early experimental school in what is now West Bengal; and at Archigram's *The Bottery*, an appropriated image, lifted from a Sony portable TV advertisement, as published in the early seventies in some glossy magazine. It is reprinted in *Concerning Archigram* (Crompton 1999), and it is used in lectures by David Greene, a founding member of the Archigram team. At first blush, these four examples do not readily cohere. However, the architectural motives for each example can be seen to provide a pre-dispositional unity of purpose across the centuries.

III Part Two: The system of the (fine) arts

Having crossed that bridge, we find ourselves in part two, Chapter 3. There, we start to look carefully at the system of the arts and at the inclusion by some (and exclusion by others) of architecture from the system of the arts. If architecture is to be considered a fine art, it must deal with the criticism that its having utility, as its principal value, debars it from inclusion. Art for Art's sake is a mantra of romantics. It is surely derived from Kant's claim that art should, whilst being purposive, yet have no determinate purpose. On the view of exclusionists, no staircase could be a work of art, or detail thereof, since its determinate purpose, of enabling vertical circulation, dominates its value, thereby subjugating design to utilitarian values. It can be beautiful; but its beauty is constrained within the criteria of its function; and functional beauty belongs to the mechanical arts.

Contrary to any such view, this book aims to provide argument that architecture is a fine art. We shall have to deal with this confrontation, and we do. In the next section of this introduction, I sidestep the question of history. This is done by referring to both Vitruvius, briefly, and Alberti in more focus. Consideration of these two thinkers provides us with the background with which to conduct our assessment of architecture within the context of the aesthetics of fine art as developed in the eighteenth century. In doing so, we treat the arguments of these historical figures as they stand before us: to be accepted or rejected by reason alone.

In Chapter 3, we shall look at the age-old, and still persistent, view that art in general, and architecture in particular, is mimetic. It is unclear as to whether Alberti subscribes to that view. His interest in mathematics shows an ancient tendency to see number and proportion as attributes of nature that might secure the basis for the beautiful in art. We shall look at the view more broadly in this chapter. We look at the recent argument that any work of fine art must belong to an art-kind that there are only works within specific kinds of art, such as painting, poetry, theatre, film, dance, music and architecture.

In Chapters 4 and 5, we encounter Kant's classification of the arts which is more than a mere taxonomy, since he provides criteria for membership to the groupings it comprises. And we shall have recourse to the notion of aesthetic ideas. These, he introduces as a distinctive mark of the fine arts.

Kant holds that the mark of artistic genius is the ability to make works independently of any rule, and yet within the confines of the discipline concerned. This needs some explanation, particularly as, on some interpretations, it looks as if he thinks that only artists who work outwith rules can truly consider themselves artists. That looks a little strict and unhelpful to those souls who have spent their lives making art – at least as we would ordinarily recognize it. Taken strictly, there would be many fewer artists, as the class would have to be revised down to count only examples of genius as works of fine art. In order to make sense of the artist's genius we shall, in turn, rely upon the notion of an *aesthetic idea*, as that is introduced in Kant's theory of fine art.

On another view, there can be artists who learn the constitutive rules of their particular art, and who practise it with proficiency, and yet do not achieve the status of genius. These artists might, for instance, learn how to make images, and then work within the styles that surround them at the time. So, some artists will become cubists, for instance, even though that work was inaugurated by Pablo Picasso and Georges Bracque. Those who follow the lead of the genius are, as it were, journeymen, and their work is valuable as it is the source of aesthetic experience to many. In Chapter 4, we look at the imagination as it is engaged in Kant's conception of cognition. This is a necessary step in our coming to grips with how the imagination works in the making and appreciation of art. Chapter 5 considers the way in which Kant employs the 'free play of imagination' in his account of fine art. From this, he develops the notion of aesthetic ideas to show the importance and special status of the fine arts.

Chapter 6 introduces, as a central problem, the issue of function in architecture. Here we consider how function has been treated as a debasement of all that is fine, in fine art. It is the utilitarian aspect of architecture that has given cause to think it less refined than the art and culture it houses. We look at one particularly well-argued case against the inclusion of architecture in the fine arts: that made by Gordon Graham in his book, *The Re-enchantment of the World: Art versus Religion* (Graham 2007). Graham calls upon the difference between the Dionysian (Nietzsche) conception of art and the Apollonian (Kant).

We turn, again to Kant, whose brief comments on architecture provide enough for us to build a case for architecture as a fine art.

IV Part Three: The medium of architecture

Chapter 7 proposes an account of the medium of architecture in line with the requirements set out in Chapters 3 and 6. The medium of architecture as a fine art is constrained by our conception of use. However, functionalism as it is standardly put forward is rejected in favour of a more liberal Kantian interpretation, which claims the function, use or purpose of a building is realization of an aesthetic idea. We shall need to look at how an adherence to Kant's conception of architecture gives licence to the architect to make works which are appreciated in terms of their function. Whilst the use constrains the work, it nevertheless does not prevent the work from realizing that use in a manner that affords aesthetic experience.

Two architectural theorists separated by a half-millennium come together to provide us with a sense of what is the work of an architect. Leon Battista Alberti and Robin Evans focus on drawing. It is here in the translation of drawing into building and back into our understanding that we are provided with an insight into the operations of design and, hence, another facet of the medium.

In Chapter 8, we proceed to examine the scale of architectural tasks. We look at the large – our encounter with the city and how our perception and imagination are engaged with it. We leave buildings behind and take to the streets of the city, where we meet *flâneurs* wandering through Paris and situationists making provocations. The city features in our lives as a collaged phenomenon. Cities have their rat-runs, squares, parks and civic buildings, as well as shops and houses. These are all encountered in walks on daily journeys to and from places of work. They are part of the furniture of our lives.

What of the dead? Cemeteries provide us with an example of how the mystery of life is ever present. We build cemeteries to memorialize our dead; to keep their memories 'alive'. This surely says something about how we conceive of ourselves as a specific type of being. It returns us to the importance of mythology.

However, just as cities are vast, so details are small. The architect has to consider her building in the context of the city and beyond. She must also reconcile the kilometres that surround her building with the millimetres of the detail without and within – the door handle, the tap, the light switch, the skirting board. From the majuscule to the miniscule, she must take responsibility for every facet of her design. The thumb groove on the banister at the Royal Festival Hall is architecturally important in its accommodation of those using the staircase. So, too, is the façade as seen from across the river at the Embankment. This is the case for architectural aesthetics; for appreciating architecture as an art.

In the concluding chapter we re-visit some of our old haunts, now armed with a view to what is the fine art of architecture. The Paris café calls to us again. We review the notion of function as it is weaved into the medium of architecture and we return gently to the good earth whereon we build our architecture.

PART ONE

The wide conversation surrounding architecture

1

Hunting and gathering

I The palaver

In Jung's memoir, especially his recollection of a journey into east Africa, he tells of the organization of the palaver. The men sit on the ground. Then one of the men gives an address, the *shauri,* in which the agenda for the palaver is delivered. He reports that often the palavers contain amusing guessing riddles, ensuring their popularity. They seldom lasted more than an hour and he gives the impression that anything can be brought to the attention of the gathered tribesmen. As I read his account, it seemed a democratic way of musing about their daily life. (Although women did not take part.) Nevertheless, it embodies the idea of a shared way of living that we shall encounter throughout. The image of Langlands & Bell's *Eclipse* occurred to me as a work of art in an architectural medium – a modern piece that embodies the idea of community.

In part one of this book, we call upon a wide range of sources in order to develop a conversation surrounding our interest in, and our preliminary conceptions of, the appreciation of architecture. Such method has a chance of keeping the text within the constraints of broad cultural understanding, both of architecture and of its origins, whilst keeping it within the confines of common sense – if it is possible to so constrain the conversation. This is a liberal, inclusive consideration of attitudes. However, its accommodation of broad opinion must not count against the provision of argument that stands to reason – argument that will eventually establish architecture as a fine art. In this preliminary palaver, as might be expected, we set about the foundations of a theory of architecture and give notice of its conclusion: that architecture is to be appreciated as a fine art.

FIGURE 1.1 *Langlands & Bell,* Eclipse, *Wood, steel, lacquer. 76 cm × 520 cm × 250 cm. (Installation view* Sitting Pretty *Belsay Hall, Northumberland, UK, 1999.) (Courtesy of the artists.)*

In this first chapter, in particular, we shall consider examples of what I shall call persuasions. These persuasions call upon our interest, not only in architecture but also in the conversational milieu that surrounds it. We shall use observation and attention *as* argument. We are attempting to do aesthetics by pointing to features of our lives that persuade us of their importance, rather than by providing strict logical arguments that lead us inexorably towards conclusions that cannot be resisted. 'Look at it like this', recommends itself in aesthetic discussions as a way of seeing the best or most promising way of experiencing the fine arts.

During what follows, we shall look closely at the thinking of those who would exclude architecture from the system of the fine arts. Some have claimed and argued that architecture, being a public art, is better understood in terms of everyday aesthetics. They argue that architecture is not a fine art. Since the central claim of this book is to the contrary, we had better be ready to meet the arguments these thinkers put forward. Therefore, we shall look at the system of the fine arts as it emerged in the eighteenth century along with its contemporary philosophical justification in aesthetics.

We shall draw upon sources across the analytic/continental divide, as well as further abroad in related disciplines. During the modern period, the arts in general have become philosophically engaged. It seems right, therefore, to observe the sources to which artists themselves have turned their attention. Artists increasingly feel the need to formulate their theoretical position within the particular art they practise. In philosophy, the analytic tradition, historically comprising mostly, though not exclusively, English-speaking philosophers, has, during its history, cocked a snook at the continental intellectual milieu. These anglophone philosophers claim that their continental counterparts erect no barriers between philosophy and the arts. No wonder that artists are more at home in the discussions arising from European sources. In Europe they have been included in the conversation.

However, English-speaking philosophers might profitably think that the literary aspect of French philosophy, for instance, far from being unwelcome in aesthetics, is an area in which the two traditions might converge to their mutual benefit. We have most certainly moved on from the attitudes encountered by Simone de Beauvoir, whilst visiting the United States, when she wrote to her lover and colleague, the French philosopher Jean-Paul Sartre, in a letter dated, 7 February 1947, wherein she bitterly complains,

> [W]e went to Jean Condit's. Arrival at 6, cocktail, then they took me to dinner and kept me till midnight. For 6 hours I argued in English, alone against them all, passionately. I was battling with [Clement] Greenberg, [William] Phillips and Phillip Rhav [editors of *Partisan Review*], and a tall, pretentious young man who says we have no right to dabble in philosophy because we don't know [Bertrand] Russell.
>
> (Beauvoir 1992, 422)

This episode is given fuller treatment in Beauvoir's journal, *America Day by Day* (Beauvoir 2000, 39–41). On the comparison of the two traditions, it is worth noting the entry in the journal for 26 April 1947, where she writes on the universities she has been visiting,

> Philosophy is not at all the broadest discipline, as it is in Germany and France; here, it is divided into completely independent branches – psychology, sociology, and logic – which are treated like exact sciences and remain as narrowly self-enclosed as physics or chemistry (...) At Yale they are seriously interested in phenomenology and in various forms of existentialism, but this instance is nearly unique.
>
> (Beauvoir 2000, 306)

Interestingly, it is at Yale school of Philosophy that Karsten Harries, the German philosopher and author of *The Ethical Function of Architecture* (1997) has found his home.

The arts, even in English-speaking countries, have been more closely linked with the philosophy of the continental tradition than with the analytic school. However, there are increasing developments, especially within aesthetics from which emerges *substantive aesthetics*; an area which sees philosophers of both traditions coming together with historians, theorists and critics; and, indeed, with practising artists themselves. Richard Wollheim's *Painting As A Art*, (Wollheim 1987) is a case in point, given as The Mellon Lectures in Washington in 1984. Indeed, Wollheim was one of the inaugural group of philosophers, art historians and practising artists who, as early as 1960, set up the British Society of Aesthetics, with its academic journal, *The British Journal of Aesthetics*. The group included Benjamin Britten, Kenneth Clark, Cecil Day Lewis, William Empson, John Gielgud, E. H. Gombrich, Yehudi Menuhin, Henry Moore, Nicholas Pevsner, Herbert Read, Sacheverell Sitwell, Basil Spence, Stephen Spender, Adrian Stokes, and Graham Sutherland, among other luminaries across the broad spectrum of the arts, art history and its philosophy.

A younger generation of aestheticians have followed this lead, and, in so doing, have worked against the continental opinion that analytical philosophers discuss, but do not engage with, the fine arts. In particular, and we shall discuss his work later, Dominic McIver Lopes has given a philosophical account of why it is that philosophers should seek to learn from artists, critics and historians; and that a conversation should be developed to include the various perspectives afforded by such a rich diversity of participants.

II Rudimentary sketch

How to begin? From where does our conception of architecture arise? It comes to us, it will be argued, from the most basic wonderment we humans feel when attempting to fit ourselves into the world. It arises, that is, from our earliest enquiries into what we are. We are reflective agents striving to accommodate the world, and to find our accommodation within it. As Harries puts it: '[Y]ou need to feel metaphysically at home' (Harries *et al* 2017, 16). I take Harries to be making a distinction between a physical location, marked out on a map by coordinates, and a place, with the stamp of habitation upon it; so that the same location might, at different times, be regarded as two different places – the one a home of the hunter gatherer, for instance, the other the home of a post-industrialist people. That is not the metaphysics of *being*, as German philosopher Martin Heidegger conceived it. It is, however, a sort of metaphysics of place – that comes up for air from the depths of *being*. It is a metaphysics of place that humanizes location – projects *our* identity across its surface. We might wonder how so.

We shall start by looking at expressions of this wonderment – as found in the autobiography of Carl Jung (Jung 2019). A pioneer of analytical psychology, he takes a journey through west Africa, from Mombassa via Nairobi through to Uganda. He finds himself distanced from the world he knows and yet strangely familiar with the timeless aspect of the world in which he finds himself. He describes a feeling of *déjà vu*, a discombobulation with this world into which he is pitched; or which, more accurately, he has pitched himself. He feels, quite reasonably, alien in this land, but he also recognizes that something in him is pre-rationally attached to its autochthony.

Jung's journal entry suggests that the bond he feels with the native African pre-dates modernity and is a primordial connection with humanity at its most general. But what is the nature of such connection, and how are we to establish our sense of belonging in the world? The problem is one that Heidegger faced in his protracted discussion of *Dasein* (being). A number of his essays are collected as *Poetry, Language, Thought* (Heidegger 2013). In 'Building, Dwelling, Thinking', he discusses the nature of dwelling and sees that as a condition in which we are to find our home. In another 'The Thing', he considers the relationship between things in the world and our finding our homes among them. Both cast light upon the nature of the origins of architecture – the primordial stuff out of which architecture has arisen.

Having looked at dwelling as the underpinning of our sense of settlement – our finding our way home – we need to turn our attention to the judgements we make about that home. Are the judgements we make about the arts, in general, objective? Standardly, student essays will proclaim that if you ask a thousand different persons to pass judgement on a work of art you will get a thousand different opinions. If that is where we were to end up, aesthetics would get nowhere. It is, however, where Scottish philosopher David Hume takes up his essay concerning the standard of taste (Hume 1985).

Hume worries about how it is that we make judgements about works of art. Having recognized that it is credible to judge one writer better than another, he wants to find the warrant of that claim. In the end it comes down to developing one's taste (one's sensitivity to the beautiful in art) over time, so that those with sufficient time (and sensitivity) to attend to art will find their refined judgements in concert with others so refined. Kant takes up the antinomy of taste – on the one hand it is essentially subjective: experiences are states of particular minds at particular times; and on the other, when we disagree over judgements of taste, we feel bound to seek resolution. Aesthetic judgements are normative. (Compare this to one person liking olives, another not. In matters of mere preferences no genuine dispute arises. Your liking for olives makes no demand upon my response to the wretched things.)

Our aesthetic judgements are such that we find their scope general, thus binding. When I claim that some object, scene or event is beautiful, I include in the judgement the claim that any other subject experiencing the object, scene or event *should* agree with me. So Kant's claim is that the judgement's scope *aims* to include us all, not that it does. It demands agreement but cannot command it. We shall discuss this in relation to works of art in general, and then works of architecture in particular, in the second part of the book. For now, let's persist with our conversation concerning architecture.

III Early intuitions

Where to begin? For a number of years, we have started the third-year architectural theory class with a question upon which finalists might have a view: 'What is architecture?'

The undergraduate students, congregating for 'History and Theory' courses, emerge from four or five different studio groups – each studio emitting a distinct whiff of architectural prejudice provided by the studio director, himself or herself, a practising architect. The studio model was borrowed from the 'atelier system' dating back to 1819 when the French Royal Architectural Academy transformed into *École des Beaux Arts*. Even after some remodelling at the radically modern Bauhaus, the studio system has survived and still embodies the standard teaching format in architecture, art and other niche courses in the visual arts and design. Art history, art theory and aesthetics more broadly leak out of (and seep into) studio practice. (As noted, Art, especially in the modern period, has become intrinsically theoretical. It is no longer possible to appreciate work of the twentieth and twenty-first century without some idea of the theoretical positions of artists and their commentators.)

In answer to my question, the students responded along party lines which fell, more or less, into two seemingly contradictory positions. The first: it is the design of buildings that adds poetry to the built environment – architectural poesy. (For my purposes, I was pleased to note *The Oxford Shorter English Dictionary* lists under Poesy, 'poetry in the concrete'.) The second: that the best architecture is engineered as a solution to building requirements as set out in the design brief. Put so, it would seem the view is at odds with fine art from the start. We shall see. But these views, thoughtful as they might have been, were hesitant. When pressed, adherents of the former view held that architecture *is* an art; of the latter, that it is more mathematical, requiring skills of calculation rather than aesthetic judgement; but that, like mathematics, it is capable of a certain manifest beauty – a sort of 'back door' aesthetics.

All seemed to think the architect provides accommodation for the lives we lead, accommodation viewed expansively to embrace anywhere that we pursue our lives. It would have to include offices, factories, warehouses, restaurants, places of worship, bars, parks, city squares and village greens. It would include airports and their lounges; stations for buses and trains; stadia, theatres, galleries, shopping malls, and indeed anything designed to adapt the environment to the purposes pursued by us in *our* world. It would include roads, road works, cars and traffic jams; pedestrians sheltering from the rain in bus shelters; and so on. (In a published interview between Archigram co-founder, David Greene and interlocutors Jon Goodbun and David Cunningham, Greene is reported to have said, 'When it's raining in Oxford Street the architecture is no more important than the rain.') (Greene et al. 2001, 198). To this extent, the students' perspectives converged on the view that dwelling and our understanding of dwelling are at the heart of the architect's work. And thus, we were prompted to read Heidegger's 'Building Dwelling Thinking', as a text that brought the various strands of our answers together. But not for long.

Heidegger begins his essay by disavowing allegiance to either of the views identified (however vaguely) by my third-year students. He writes, and thereby cautions my students, that his task is not to provide a recipe book, adherence to which will guarantee the production of good architecture:

> This thinking about building does not presume to discover architectural ideas, let alone to give rules for building. This venture in thought does not view building as an art or as a technique of construction; rather it traces building back into that domain to which everything that *is* belongs. We ask:
>
> 1 What is it to dwell?
>
> 2 How does building belong to dwelling? (Heidegger 2013, 144)

Heidegger's answers are prolonged and tortuous, occasionally tenuous. Nevertheless, his thinking about building leads us to a point upon which we might draw the two camps together, even if we have to separate them at a later stage. His answer to Question 1 is something like 'living well' or flourishing; or, more Heideggerian perhaps, 'being'; 'to dwell' is 'to live well' or 'to flourish', or 'to be'. And this 'being' is connected to building. In answer to Question 2, building belongs to dwelling by way of our habitation of the world, more specifically *our* world. (There remains a question of just exactly who *we* are.) Building, for Heidegger, means tending to the world, preserving it and living in peace with our neighbours in harmony and conformity. Inhabitation is the extension of ourselves into the world, so that the world is seen as both my world and a world shared with others like me. The world is where I am situated amongst others, just as I am a being in the world in which they find themselves situated.

Heidegger's essay entitled 'The Thing' (Heidegger 2013) was given as a lecture in 1950 and published as 'Das Ding' in 1951. In it he talks about our relation to objects in the world. He is thinking about artefacts and our relationship to them. 'Building Dwelling Thinking' focuses upon the nature of dwelling and so considers our being in the world. 'The Thing' considers what it is for us to be among things and how those things comprise a world in which we are situated. Both essays are later Heidegger, but both exhibit his distinction between 'present-at-hand' and 'ready-to-hand'. Works of architecture, amongst other *useful* artefacts, are 'ready-to-hand'. At least while they are operational within the scope of our lives. Once ruined or broken, they return to their status as 'present-at-hand'; no longer reached for but instead intruding upon our lives as in need of repair. English philosopher Simon Critchley draws the comparison,

> Heidegger introduces a distinction between two ways of approaching the world: the present-at-hand (*Vorhandenheit*) and the ready-to-hand (*Zuhandenheit*). Present-at-hand refers to our theoretical apprehension of a world made up of objects. It is the conception of the world from which science begins. The ready-to-hand describes our practical relation to things that are handy or useful. Heidegger's basic claim is that practice precedes theory, and that the ready-to-hand is prior to the present-at-hand (...) Furthermore, the world is not simply full of handy, familiar meaningful things. It is also full of persons. If I am fundamentally with my world, then that world is a common world that is experienced together with others.
>
> (Critchley 2009)

Dwelling relates us to the world in such a way as to operate within it as participants. In so establishing such a relation the world is present to us as a ground for practical purposes. But the question persists as to who *we* are?

In 'The Thing', Martin Heidegger's essay concerning the nature of things – *as-they-are-in-themselves* – we are treated to a poetic meditation on a clay jug. First of all the potter selects and prepares a piece of earth. This clay is then shaped by the potter to be a self-standing jug, a vessel that is filled, and in turn fills other vessels. So, the process of making the jug is determined by our conception of the place the jug must hold in our lives.

> The giving of the outpouring can be a drink. The outpouring gives water, it gives wine to drink.
>
> The spring stays on in the water of the gift. In the spring the rock dwells, and in the rock dwells the dark slumber of the earth, which receives the rain and dew of the sky. In the water of the spring dwells the marriage of sky and earth. It stays in the wine given by the fruit of the vine, the fruit in which the earth's nourishment and the sky's sun are betrothed to one another. In the gift of water, in the gift of wine, sky and earth dwell. But the gift of the outpouring is what makes the jug a jug. In the jugness of the jug, sky and earth dwell.
>
> The gift of the pouring out is drink for mortals. It quenches their thirst. It refreshes their leisure. It enlivens their conviviality. But the jug's gift is at times also given for consecration. If the pouring is for consecration, then it does not still a thirst. It stills and elevates the celebration of the feast.
>
> (Heidegger 2013, 170)

The wine in the jug is our grasping at the vine which grew out of the earth, nurtured by the sun under the sky. It has been processed by us from grape to elixir, so that both jug and wine symbolize our dwelling *in* the world.

We can imagine the jug being the topic of a piece of prose poetry by Francis Ponge who might recognize this intense focusing upon the ordinariness of things. In recognizing the quotidian stillness and quietness of things, they become marvellous. Ponge's poetry itself seems to single out the strangeness of – well – *things*. And this strangeness includes us.

Noticing this strangeness is a move towards *grasping* what it is that we are, and *seeing* that architecture, like the jug, is important evidence of our coming into contact with the world.

Ponge is one influence, amongst others, on contemporary concrete artist, Jane Bustin's practice, and her work often takes one of his poems and then makes a 'something' that suggests the 'somethings' he writes about (Bustin 2014). The scorched silk with its darkened edge readily brings to mind the mantle or pallium of an oyster, its strange slimy burnt-umber hem from which we might ordinarily recoil. (We have to learn to enjoy oysters; to be *at home* eating them.) Bustin's work uses a poetic sensitivity to the nature of the materials she fetches to a work. Her sensitivity calls upon us, as does Ponge's poetry, to look more intensely at the things in it and at their qualities. In so noticing these qualities, we become accustomed to them. It is in such observations of things that we see their simple beauty, and we feel that their presentation to us is a shared experience of that beauty. The works seem to call to us. Concrete Art forbids us to pass through its material quality in order to reach some content beyond. It presents itself 'simply' as a material object of beauty. It sets itself against the tradition of representation in the visual arts.

FIGURE 1.2 *Jane Bustin,* Tablet II, *2014, mixed media. (Courtesy of the artist).*

Concrete Art rejects the premise that the visual arts are representational in essence. Rather, it calls attention to the nature of the stuff from which the work is made. In this, it aligns itself with architecture, at least insofar as *some* architects have rejected the view that architecture is mimetic. (We shall come onto this conception of architecture below.) This alignment of Concrete Art with architecture is modernist in its conception, and Heidegger's essay, 'The Thing' is a source for the discussion of how we might treat the architectural within the broader visual arts that steer themselves away from mimesis. (We shall return to related problems when we move on to discuss the nature of medium specificity for art-kinds in part two of the book.)

IV Who, perhaps what, are we?

How should one identify oneself, and with whom? Writing, in his autobiography, of a journey between Mombassa and Nairobi, undertaken in the Autumn of 1925, Jung captures a sense of timeless belonging that he *feels* in a strange encounter with a Maasai warrior he sees from the train window at daybreak:

> On a jagged rock above us a slim, brownish-black figure stood motionless, leaning on a long spear, looking down at the train (…)
>
> I was enchanted by this sight – it was a picture of something utterly alien and outside my experience, but on the other hand a most intense *sentiment du déjà vu*. I had the feeling that I had already experienced this moment and had always known this world which was separated from me only by distance in time. It was as if I were this moment returning to the land of my youth, and as if I knew that dark skinned man who had been waiting for me for five thousand years (…)
>
> I could not guess what string within myself was plucked at the sight of that solitary dark hunter. I knew only that his world had been mine for countless millenia (…)
>
> (Jung 2019, 302–3)

The 'plucking of a string' and the feeling of *déjà vu* situate Jung in a world that '*had been*' his. The comment is of interest to anyone whose concerns meet at the intersection of psychology, anthropology and philosophy. Psychology – what is going on in the mind of someone like Jung when he undergoes such an experience; Anthropology – what is timeless, autochthonous, about the Maasai way of life that shows something to Jung about our living on this earth or being situated in it; Philosophy – what, at its most general, does the feeling *mean* for someone, such as Jung, to be so situated, away from his or her contingent form of life?

In plucking the string a chord is struck; and that chord is a *felt* harmony that vibrates between the ancient world of the Maasai and the world of the 'enlightened' modern European. It signals an entrenched unity that spans the vast divides of time and space, and it discovers in that unity a cousinage, if not a brotherhood of man.

The occasion of Jung's being overseen by the tribesman and the gaze returned in wonder is conditioned by an emblem of the Industrial Revolution, itself born of enlightenment science and the philosophy from which that science is underpinned. Modernity placed a premium upon reason. Concomitantly, suspicion of myth looked to replace all things of which we are uncertain with scientifically rigorous explanations. Thus, we find that Western industrialized modern cultures are at odds with those pre-modern cultures whose continuous belief in myths strikes the modern as superstitious.

We can only ponder what the Maasai tribesman made of the steam engine rattling and clattering its carriages through his land. What brought the psychoanalytic pioneer and the warrior into each other's orbit is precisely what secured their independent perspectives. Industrialism and its consequences – simultaneously introduced and removed Jung, to and from the world in which the tribesman *lived*. The world upon which Jung directed his gaze was the mythical world of eternal innocence – one of harmony and peace. His feeling of 'intense *sentiment du déjà vu*' is uncanny (our usual translation of the German, 'unheimlich' – more strictly translated as 'unhomely'). In Jung, as in so many modernist writings, we find alienation articulated, a confused emotion expressed if not explained. As we shall see, this alienation, and the longing attendant upon it, is a feeling of exile; a feeling of 'not-belonging'; and a yearning for some mythological account or a search for a scientific explanation, either of which might make sense of it. We seek to flourish and to build our appreciation of flourishing into our culture.

The autobiographical note also reveals the accord with which each of these individuals engages life. For neither man is nature to be considered merely dumb and brutal. Each is bound to seek meaning in life, both eschewing the chaos of a world ungoverned by narratives that seek to explain our inhabitation of this place. Jung says that he is looking for a mythology of his own; without which, the world appears governed as if by clockwork. He is in search of a narrative that will explain to *him* the nature of *his* attachment to the world. It is in his ability to bear witness that he finds this meaning. The act of bearing witness means, for Jung, that humanity itself 'co-creates' the world; that God needs humanity for His creation to exist.

Bearing witness, we might think, is the least we can do. It is in the epiphanies of the everyday that we come to value our lives, and it is but a short stretch from that to think that our response to the arts is as witness to the beauties they sensitize and alert us to. This is the simplicity and the beauty that is to be found in artists such as Jane Bustin, and it is at the heart of Heidegger's thinking in 'The Thing'.

Earlier in his book, Jung says that he read and was greatly influenced by Kant as a schoolboy, complaining that when he undertook his university education in medicine, he was restricted to reading Kant only on Sundays. (I leave it to the reader to decide whether or not reading Kant on the Sabbath is a good thing.)

If his account of the east African journey provides abstraction, then it does so in a way that, we might think, shows how broadly we should take Kant's careful consideration of the notion of a *sensus communis*. In distancing himself from the usual usage, whereby we translate from the Latin to 'common sense', Kant defends Hume against his detractors. Comparing Hume's scepticism towards our conception of causation with criticism of Hume by one of his contemporaries, Kant has this to say,

> [T]he opponents of (…) [Hume] would have had to penetrate very deeply into the nature of reason so far as it is occupied solely with pure thought, something that did not suit them. They therefore found a more expedient means to be obstinate without any insight, namely, the appeal to *ordinary common sense*. It is in fact a great gift from heaven to possess right (…) common sense. But it must be proven through deeds, by the considered and reasoned things one thinks and says, and not by appealing

> to it as an oracle when one knows of nothing clever to advance in one's defense. To appeal to ordinary common sense when insight and science run short, and not before, is one of the subtle discoveries of recent times, whereby the dullest windbag can confidently take on the most profound thinker and hold his own with him (...) [C]ommon sense and speculative understanding are both useful, but each in its own way; the one, when it is a matter of judgments that find their immediate application in experience, the other, however, when judgments are to be made in a universal mode, out of mere concepts, as in metaphysics (...)
> (Kant 2004, 9–10)

In his essay on the influence of Kant upon Jung, Andrew Samuels states that it is the archetypes in Jung that correspond to the categories in Kant (Samuels 1986). That seems a bit of a stretch. However, if we wanted to think (relatedly) in terms of the abstract unity we seek across humanity when considering architecture – we might rather consider Jung's collective unconscious and Kant's *sensus communis*.

Thus, when philosophers and anthropologists speak glowingly of 'the hearth', we see at once a unifying feature of *home* across humanity. We might put it that we are – as a species – predisposed to gather round the hearth where we are warmed and lit, and where our communal meal is prepared.

The search for narrative and, through it, mythological explanation seals us into a world of appearances at the cost of metaphysical realism. We appear to withdraw from engagement with the world described by science. On the one hand, we recognize that ibuprofen will reduce inflammation and thereby reduce our pain. Science tells us that. On the other hand, your owing me ten shillings and my demand for its repayment seems to escape any such explanation. Ibuprofen belongs to the world of science and its explanatory system. No amount of scientific evidence from the world of physics could persuade you to give me back the ten bob, nor could it persuade me to erase the debt. Generosity and obligation belong to the human world in a way that ibuprofen does not. How can we reconcile ourselves with this cleavage? One option is to include the world of science within the human world.

The hadron collider at CERN, where sub-atomic particles accelerate around a circuit in Switzerland, deliberately set up so

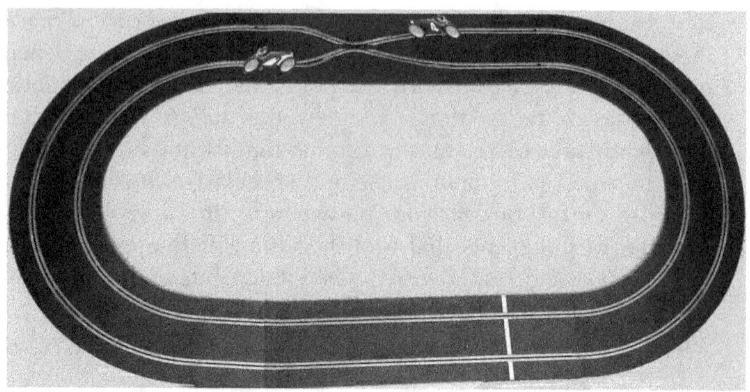

FIGURE 1.3 *Edward Winters,* Slot Car Racing: Large Hadron Collider Explained, *2022, Collage.*

as they crash into each other, is like slot car racing on acid: the toy cars scaled down to the size of sub-atomic particles, the 3 or 4 metre length of the plastic slotted track scaled up to 27 kilometres of superconducting magnets, around which, the sub-atomic particles whizz and collide.

The *human* world is occupied only by medium-sized objects. Without contesting the truth of this, we must note that medium-sized, *observable*, objects have become yet more miniscule at one end of the spectrum and yet more immense at the other. The observable world now includes sub-atomic particles. It also includes very large objects. New nebulae extend the middle-sized to include the vast *observable* stretches of outer space – to its furthest reaches, where we might only speculate what it might be to inhabit its places; to fantasize about its being 'present-at-hand' or 'ready-to-hand'. Nevertheless, we can observe those far off things by means of calculation and direct observation by The European – Extremely Large Telescope (ELT), currently under construction in the Atacama Desert in Chile. Aided by this prosthetic device, we can *see* primordial stars, galaxies, black holes and their relationships. Truly marvelous.

Earlier, as a rather lame joke, I included an image of slot car racing as an explanation of the goings-on at CERN. Notwithstanding its lameness, the image could be used to illuminate the point under consideration. Jet airplane travel has made the world much, much smaller, but Large Hadron Collider has made the millimetre much, much larger.

CERN reopened in April 2022, after three years of development. One professor, interviewed by the BBC, said they would now be looking out for 'new *phenomena*'. That is what I mean by the elasticity of 'middle-sized objects'. When Kant was setting out his arguments about the constraints of experience, he could not possibly have foretold the smallness of things we can now 'observe', nor of the vastness of things available to us through electro-telescopy. So, dark matter is now 'observable' or soon shall be. That alters the way we look at things. Kant, I assume, would agree.

Whatever elasticity we discover in our conception of 'middle-sized' objects, we need not reject the view that *our world* is delimited by the condition of observability. Observability, here, is to be understood in terms of Heidegger's 'ready-to-hand' and 'present-at-hand'. All of this amounts to our wrestling to discover the world and to find in it our place.

Dwelling is the condition of finding ourselves thrown into the world, and of our subsequent search for accommodation therein.

V War and peace 1

It is interesting that Heidegger puts such emphasis on peace. For it is only when we live in peace with our neighbours that we are at home, and thereby dwell. So, dwelling is a manner of living well, or of flourishing. How then does architecture relate to dwelling?

Let us consider, by contraposition, the opposite of living well – the opposite of flourishing; living without peace in a time of conflict; suffering the absence of home. For, if dwelling requires peace, we might consider what living without peace might mean. In one of his essays, Sartre draws attention to the privation of 'dwelling' for Parisians in Paris during the period of its Nazi occupation, 1940–4,

> You would phone a friend one day and the telephone would ring and ring in the empty apartment; you would ring his doorbell and he wouldn't come to the door; if the concierge broke in, you would find two chairs drawn up together in the hallway with German cigarette ends between the legs.
>
> (Sartre 2017, 15)

In his essay, Sartre describes a collective life *endured* under quarantine – a prolonged period of waiting in the absence of dwelling, merely existing, in the hope of its return. It is as if dwelling has been set aside, mothballed, 'meantimed'. The wait is a protracted removal from what we regard as home. Sartre was not only a philosopher, but also a novelist, playwright and essayist; and it is, therefore, unsurprising that the passage above is so imagistic, almost filmic, in the atmosphere educed. It is also a refusal of the architectural, in that we are drawn into a consideration of how the hallway has been rendered hostile, sickening, repulsive. It is alienation expressed. Sartre shows us what it is to be an exile in one's own city.

What happened in that Parisian hallway is queer, unsettling; or, *unheimlich*. And so, it is possible, in such circumstances, real or imagined, to think of our lives unfolded in buildings and in cities regardless of the architecture in which they are embodied. That said – and the example, though real, is admittedly extreme – the terrible existence during such a period cannot be conceived as *dwelling*. It is precisely 'not-living-well'.

Another example, this time from John Steinbeck's *A Russian Journal*, describes Stalingrad in 1949. It is a piece of writing that again shows how we might live if we are deprived of the circumstances of living in peace, harmony and conformity with our neighbours. It underlies the importance of *dwelling* as a condition of what we might ask of architecture, by showing us what it is like to live *without dwelling* in Heidegger's sense:

> Our windows looked out on acres of rubble, broken brick and concrete and pulverised plaster, and in the wreckage the strange dark weeds that always seem to grow in destroyed places (…) Underneath the rubble were cellars and holes, and in these holes people lived (…) We would watch out of the window of our room, and from behind a slightly larger pile of rubble would suddenly appear a girl, going to work in the morning, putting the last little touches to her hair with a comb. She would swing out through the weeds on her way to work (…) It was a strange and heroic travesty on modern living.
>
> (Steinbeck 1987, 652)

Steinbeck records his amazement at the ability to sustain something of a way of life amongst the destitution brought about by war. In the same piece he goes on to write of a young woman who was unable to so do:

> Somewhere in the terror of the fighting in the city, something had snapped, and she retired to some comfort of forgetfulness (...) [O]ne morning I saw a woman coming out of another hole and give her half a loaf of bread (...) She looked like a half-wild dog at the woman who had given her the bread, and watched her suspiciously until she had gone back to her own cellar (...)
>
> We wondered how many there might be like this, minds that could not tolerate living in the twentieth century any more, that had retired (...) to the ancient hills of the human past, into the old wilderness of pleasure and pain, and self-preservation.
>
> (Steinbeck 1987, 653)

So, by contraposition, dwelling is what surmounts these terrible conditions of the 'old wilderness' from which we have emerged, protecting us from them by means of peaceful assembly, free congregation, belonging. And so, Steinbeck cautions against a return to the 'ancient hills of the human past', choosing civilization over an unsocialized nihilism of the kind encountered during war. Incarcerated by the parentheses of war we are, thereby, devoid of the comforts of home.

Having found ourselves in the world, we seek to establish ourselves in relation to our kind, thereby forging an identity. We seek to dwell in peace with our neighbours. Should we fail, we are distressed, discomfited, de-humanized, 'un-homed'.

VI Dwelling: A naturalistic account?

A question arises. If dwelling is essential to architecture – and if dwelling is co-descriptive with flourishing – is dwelling, then, pre-rational, primordial? Were cave-dwellers doing something like architecture when they adapted caves to their purposes? Are beavers builders of dams; birds designers of nests; badgers of sets? If the answer to any of these questions is 'Yes', then it looks highly likely that our conception of architecture has been naturalized to such an extent that it is precluded from consideration as a fine art.

For beavers, birds and badgers do not participate in any of the other arts. They make neither paintings nor sculptures; none write symphonies or operas; and birds, renowned for their song, do not sing.

It is true that cave dwellers made images in the caves they inhabited, but these images are to painting what caves are to architecture. They pre-figure the arts we now consider central to our culture. They are, as it were, substrates of the arts we now practise and enjoy. We might look upon them as primitive forms or quasi-arts, out of which the arts we practise have emerged. They are, so to speak, *Ur-arts*.

Cave-dwellers did not dwell; not, at least, in the sense in which that concept is being introduced here as foundational to our understanding of architecture. Beavers, birds and badgers do not engage in critical review, nor do they squabble about the *aesthetic* character of their dams, nests or sets. The question of the relationship between dwelling and architecture persists in our fitting the latter within the framework of the former. We might say that 'dwelling' has developed into a cultural practice. The art of architecture has arisen out of our fastening critical aesthetic projections onto the 'lived world' in which we (*naturally*?) accommodate ourselves.

We could put it that in considering *Ur-architecture*, we get a sense of that upon which our need for contemporary architecture is founded. This, too, helps to explain why it is that Heidegger was so reluctant to pursue the quest to establish rules of architecture. For 'dwelling' is logically antecedent to, and foundational for, the art that is to be built upon it.

In her recent autobiographical book, *The See-Through House: My Father in Full Colour*, Shelley Klein describes the house in which she grew up, *High Sunderland*, a modernist house commissioned by her father, the fabric and fashion designer, Bernat Klein. Klein senior regarded the house as a work of art. (It is.) However, he forbade the usual constraints that might be put upon a work of a particular art-kind. He treated the house as a formal composition, in a purely abstract appraisal, and not as a work of architecture. Consequently, Shelley Klein was not permitted to have a Christmas tree when she was a girl, nor was she allowed to put her plants on the windowsills when she returned from university as a young woman. In each case the reason given was that these would intrude upon the formal beauty of the house. They would ruin it as a work of art.

FIGURE 1.4 *Peter Womersley,* High Sunderland, *1958. © Tom Parnell 2016.*

Here, in discussing a piece of furniture in the hallway upon which no one was to be seated, she neatly captures the aesthetic view to which her father subscribed,

> [A] chair by the Danish designer Poul Kjærholm, is an exercise in frugality. Known as PK25, it is typical of all Kjærholm's work being a simple combination of steel and braided halyard (…) It is a surprisingly comfortable chair, although if you are over the age of forty-five or thereabouts, it is impossible to get up from without help of some kind because the seat is nearly at floor level. This, however, is a minor drawback compared to the chair's beauty; besides which, nobody actually sits on it because chairs of this type are not really for sitting on (…) [I]n reality this chair was not a chair. It was a sculpture.
>
> (Klein 2020, 19–21)

The aesthetic commitment of both Bernat Klein and his daughter (now accommodated to the house and sensitized to her father's

FIGURE 1.5 *Poul Kjæholm,* PK25, *Chair prototype, 1951. © Ramblersen2, 2018.*

vision) clearly put formal beauty above any conception of what the object is meant to be: a chair; or, indeed, with respect to *High Sunderland*: a house.

This surely pulls into focus two important points concerning the aesthetics of fine art that we shall need to discuss in more detail below. The first is the nature of an art-kind – how do we determine what constraints are to be put upon the various art-kinds? To wit: what is it in virtue of which a painting is a painting; a poem is a poem; a sculpture: a sculpture; a work of architecture: architecture, etc., etc.?

The second point is the connection between beauty in design (generally) and function. Does function exercise any criterial constraint over the *appearance* of designed objects? And, if so, how? Klein senior and his daughter deny the constraint and do so on the premise that as an art work simpliciter, the formal beauty of the chair (and the house) overrides any such art-kind constraints.

This is important for us. When we come to consider the 'System of the Arts', in Chapter 3, we shall address the problem of unity across the arts. Eventually, we shall have to ask if there is anything that secures 'fine-art-hood' to a purported art-kind. Here, early on, we have an example of a modernist optimism that art is unified in its formal essence.

Shelley Klein's disappointment, at being denied a Christmas tree and being forbidden to clutter the windowsills with plants, is assuaged by her feeling at home in her family house. Here she writes about her attachment to *High Sunderland*:

> How can I move on from this house, the house I grew up in, the house where I spent all of my formative years? What is it about High Sunderland and about Beri [Bernat] that keeps me clinging on as if my life depends on it?
>
> In Scotland there's a term used by farmers called 'hefting', derived from the Old Norse word 'heft' meaning 'to bind'(...) Sheep that are hefted are said to belong to the landscape in that they carry within them an instinctive understanding of their surroundings. They know where the best places are to take shelter, where they need to avoid because of bogs or cliffs, where the best grazing lies (...) Over the years the land becomes mapped in their blood (...)
>
> I am hefted to High Sunderland. The house lies in my blood (...)
>
> But is it rational to feel like this? About a building? Surely a house is just a volume of space enclosed by bricks and mortar or, in this case, glass.
>
> (Klein 2020, 13–14)

In this passage, she describes her relationship to the house in a way that recalls Heidegger's conception of dwelling, before tentatively questioning that feeling because of the puzzle emanating from it. But we are in a position to re-assure her. Houses are surely not just volumes of space enclosed by bricks and mortar, or glass. The naïve optimism of modernist formalism is rejected, thus far, on the grounds that such formalism immunizes the house from its required purpose: to accommodate our dwelling. In Chapter 3, we will consider the argument that any work of fine art requires to be regarded within the context provided by the medium of some specific art-kind.

Shelley Klein leaves the rational claims of aesthetics behind and dips her toe into the primordial depths in which Heidegger swims. Heidegger, in puzzling over dwelling, warned us that we would not find in his conclusions any architectural ideas, nor any rules for building. He advises that in his considerations he is not concerned with architecture as an art. As such, he too leaves the search for aesthetic reason behind or above, as he advances or delves deeper into the metaphysics of human *being*. He nevertheless identifies an important feature of architecture – that it is concerned with the making of a home to which we belong.

Of course, we can, and sometime do, live in environments that are beneath the status of architecture, as do beavers, birds and badgers; as did the women described by Steinbeck in his journal. Those women who washed and tidied themselves before setting off for work were, as we noted above, existing in parentheses – a 'no-man's-land' of mere existence. The poor soul, clutching the bread she had been given, looking 'as if she were a half-wild dog', whilst scrutinizing her benefactor, had forsaken her humanity, withdrawn from her rational nature and returned to some primitive condition.

Like the women who held onto their reason, we could return to caves (or their modern-day equivalent) and find ourselves (pre-aesthetically) accommodated. But this would be a regression that would only show that living in peace is the foundation of dwelling as that is recruited to our building an architecture of home.

In the art of architecture, 'dwelling' has been conscripted to the task of supporting 'living well', and living well is to live a full life including the development of, and sensitivity to, aesthetic experience.

It is fundamental to our development of the art of architecture – and through that development we reconcile the art to its pre-rational origin in our human condition – that we see it as emergent from that condition; but the two should be seen as bound together in a single indivisible means of inhabiting our shared world. The art of architecture arises from our natural need for shelter and security, and it is the embellishment of that need projected onto our lived environment. As in the other fine arts, architecture is expressive in that it ministers to our sense of what we are as a community with a shared *sensus communis*.

To demonstrate this, we might reconsider an exception that proves the rule. Hefting is one thing. *High Sunderland*, with its unoccupied *PK25* is another. The fine arts should not be considered as works of art simpliciter. Each work demands a conception of the art-kind to which it belongs. The conception of the art-kind (its medium specification) governs the production of each work (of whatever kind), and regulates the aesthetic response appropriate to it. *PK25* is not a sculpture and to say that it is misconceives the nature of it as a work of furniture design.

For now, we can say that the relationship between dwelling and architecture is one of internal logic: dwelling is the pre-condition for architecture and not its guarantee. More formally, dwelling is a necessary but not a sufficient condition of architecture.

VII Poetry and engineering

Let us return to the two main answers given by the undergraduate architecture students: (1) Architecture is a poetic form of building. (2) In opposition to this, architecture is the engineered solution to the problem of building. Why might there be a tension between these two views? There is. Or, perhaps more precisely, there has been. If we look at contemporary reactions to the building of the Eiffel Tower, that emblem of Paris, nowadays visited by twice the number of tourists than those who visit The Louvre, it was not always so. When Gustav Eiffel built his famous tower, it caused outrage. However, unlike today's popular indignation, aroused and then reported in the popular press, the outrage was expressed by artists and men of cultural accomplishment in Paris at the time (Hume's gentlemen of refined taste):

> The protesters conclude by mocking this 'tower of ridiculous vertiginous height,' dominating Paris just like '*a gigantic black factory chimney*,' spreading across the whole city '*like a dark ink stain, the odious shadow of this odious column of bolted metal.*'

> (…) The writers also continued to hurl insults, like Léon Bloy (‘*this truly tragic street lamp*’), Paul Verlaine (‘*this belfry skeleton*’), Francois Coppée again (‘*this mast of iron gymnasium apparatus, incomplete, confused and deformed*’), [Guy de] Maupassant encore (‘*this high and skinny pyramid of iron ladders, this giant ungainly skeleton*’), Joris-Karl Huysmans (‘*this hideous column with railings, this infundibuliform chicken wire, glory to the wire and the slab, arrow of Notre-Dame of bric-a-brac*’). Champ de Mars residents also filed a lawsuit against Eiffel.
>
> (Lemoine 2019)

The artists of Paris begrudged the ugliness of mere engineering – its lacking taste and refinement. These voices are clearly heard announcing a unified aesthetic response to the tower. Guy de Maupassant went as far as to claim that he ate at its first level café each lunchtime. It was the only place in the city he didn’t have to look at it. Eiffel responded to the signatories,

> *Are we to believe that because one is an engineer one is not preoccupied with the beauty in one’s constructions, or that one does not seek to create elegance as well as solidity as well as durability? Is it not true that the very conditions which give strength also conform to the hidden rules of harmony?*
>
> (Lemoine 2019)

Eiffel’s reply is interesting in that he *sees* the construction as a form of beauty discovered in the process of making the tower. Are there ‘hidden rules of harmony’ that might be so discovered? Why would visual beauty be hidden in the first place? Why is it not just there on the surface immediately seen by anyone with eyes (even if it requires refined taste, surely the rules of harmony are not then hidden)? One thing that we should note straight off is that Eiffel regards his construction as belonging within the aesthetic and does not offer an alternative system of value. That might be because the Eiffel Tower is, to all intents and purposes, non-functional. So the defence can hardly claim that its value lies in its fulfilment of a purpose. Indeed the ‘insults’ of the writers tend to liken it to existing functional objects whose appearance might be thought secondary to their utility. The Parisian landmark serves no specific function. Rather, it is merely a tourist attraction, to be seen as a contemporary feat of engineering, even as it has no other purpose. Yet, the tower is likened to a 'truly tragic street lamp', a 'belfry skeleton', a 'mast of iron gymnasium apparatus', a 'high and skinny pyramid of iron ladders' and a 'hideous column with railings'. All of these invoke functional objects and bring to mind the clutter that surrounds our everyday commerce. The French *aesthetes* bring attention to the freedom of art from purpose, suggesting the view that fine art is independent of utility. Eiffel similarly avoids any claims to the effect that his tower is functional. He does value 'solidity' and 'durability' – but these properties are substrates that are required for both painting and sculpture and so ought not to count as functional components in the scheme, unless some *further* account can be made of their *aesthetic* contribution to the design of the tower.

However, the contemporary controversy surrounding the tower moves away from our mooted binary opposition: the poetic art of architecture *versus* the engineered solution to construction. Eiffel's response sees engineering, especially as exemplified in the case of his tower, as one way of achieving beauty; and so, presumably, he is arguing that engineering, in general, is one method of producing a work of art, even if only through the tradesman's entrance.

Perhaps, we could be better focused if we took an example of engineering, where function *is* to the fore; so that there is no doubt that the construction is meant to engineer a solution to a practical problem. A central case in point might be Thomas Farnolls Pritchard's *Ironbridge*, in the town of that name in Shropshire, UK. The bridge in question was the first iron bridge in the world and was built to celebrate the newly developed method of making cast iron by coke smelting. It marked the beginnings of the Industrial Revolution. Pritchard's bridge, like Eiffel Tower, is, therefore, an emblem; and Pritchard was an architect and interior designer, as well as an engineer. Nevertheless, the bridge had a function – *as a bridge*. For now, we leave it as the opening of a question concerning function, aesthetic value and their connection in our understanding of architecture. We shall return to this example when considering the role of function in our appreciation of architecture in Chapter 6.

'A truly tragic street lamp.' In what follows we shall look at how architecture, the art of building, trickles down into the philosophy of design more generally. Not, however, to show that architecture is the pinnacle of what we now regard as the design arts, but to show that dwelling, the substrate of architecture, also funds the detail

FIGURE 1.6 *Thomas Farnolls Pritchard, Ironbridge, 1779.* © The Ironbridge, Ironbridge *by Richard Cooke, 2010.*

of the designed world we inhabit. It is for this reason that Roger Scruton directs so much of his attention to everyday experience of the environment and why he was at pains to write about street furniture. The experience he identifies in an article is articulated as a failing of modernism, a betrayal of that which is traditionally held dear to the community:

> Modern street lighting is totalitarian, Orwellian; everything beneath it is pallid and impersonal. When people are allowed to choose their townscape, they frequently insist that gas lamps be retained, or replaced by electric lamps that copy traditional forms and soften the street with a familiar chiaroscuro.
>
> (Scruton 1996)

Counterpose this with Maupassant's experience of electric street lighting in his short story, The Night:

> I reached the Champs-Élysées, where the cafes-concerts seemed to glow like so many hearths amid the foliage. The chestnut

> trees, smeared with yellow light, seemed painted; they looked phosphorescent. And the electric globes, like pale but brilliant moons or lunar eggs fallen from the sky or monstrous living pearls, made the dirty, ugly gas filaments and the garlands of coloured glass pale beneath their mysterious, regal, pearly brightness.
>
> (Maupassant 2017, 84–5)

In these contrasting ways of experiencing the street's illumination by gaslight, the two authors provide descriptions which are suggestive of the way in which we, fellow dwellers, might be urged to best engage with our environment. Each suggestion seems motivated by a world view as, I believe, were the two positions occupied by the students when attempting to answer the question, 'What is architecture?'

In the streetlamp case, the two opposing views might well be summed up as being motivated by the forward-looking view of the modernist, Maupassant; and the nostalgic view of the anti-modernist, Scruton. Maupassant wants the 'regal pearly brightness' of the modern lighting, especially when compared to the 'dirty, ugly gas filaments'. Scruton prefers the 'chiaroscuro' of the gas lamp or its imitation. Both writers can bring further evidence in support of their aesthetic response. Maupassant could now mention the chiaroscuro of David Lean's *The Third* Man, where Orson Welles' Harry Lime lurks in the shadows and lives in the sewers. Scruton can point to the cosy dark interiors of Amsterdam's dark bars or, more likely, the solemn interiors of candle-lit churches in mid-winter. Each of them would be gathering cases that attempt to persuade us; and each, in my view, has something to be said for it. So, these two views pull in different directions; but, at least, they both belong *within* the realm of aesthetics.

Aesthetic response engenders persuasive reason-giving. Since these reasons aim at experiences rather than truth, it is the mark of these experiences that they can be justified but not proven. That persuasion lacks compulsion does not detract from the reason-giving grounds for each judgement. It demonstrates these judgements aim at a different kind of objectivity from either practical reason: aiming at right action or pure reason, aiming at truth.

VIII The contrasting temperaments

Such contrasting views are outlined in Alan Jacobs' introduction to W. H. Auden's book-length poem, *The Age of Anxiety*. Auden believed the human condition is the result of our fall from grace. In order to address this condition there are, in each of us, two competing inclinations.

> One way to confront this predicament is to seek a return to an innocent past; another is to press forward to a perfected future. Auden called these opposing inclinations Arcadian and Utopian, and discerned in them a strict temperamental divide.
>
> (Jacobs 2011, xxi)

Arcadians wish to restore the grandeur of a past now re-imagined in daydreams. Utopians, by contrast, want to create a new and better future, a future designed to cope with whatever it is that causes our unease with present circumstances. For Arcadians, the search for grace, once our fortunate condition, is now objectified in descriptions of ideal worlds from which we have been removed. On the other hand, the Utopians' search for solutions to our current predicament is equally objectified in descriptions of ideal worlds towards which we must strive in hope.

The book involves four characters who meet by chance in a Third Avenue, New York bar during the latter stages of the Second World War. They are Malin, a Medical Intelligence Officer; Rosetta, a buyer for a department store; Emble, a sophomore attached to the U.S. Navy; and Quant, an ageing clerk. Almost as a stage direction, the characters are introduced to us, and Rosetta embarks upon an internal monologue.

Auden identified himself with the Arcadians. Evidence of the Arcadian vision is provided by Rosetta. Before meeting the others, she is drinking in the bar and thinking through her situation. In this prose passage of the poem, she laments her thwarted ambition, expressed as a yearning for a life in which she is married but which seems so remote. Those she wants to marry show no interest in her, whilst those who would marry her do not appeal. Through this asymmetry, Auden shows, also, that Rosetta sees herself as having failed. Her immediate situation, in the bar, is itself a failure as she nurses a drink and longs for the fantasy world she knows she can never attain. Rosetta is accustomed to drinking and is experienced with men. Hers is a world in which the innocence for which she longs is no longer available.

Compare this to Scruton's defence of the picture-postcard image of the countryside, in which we are to be persuaded to *see* the Arcadian value of Gilbert Scott's telephone booth. Scruton describes its design at some length before going on to place it in a country landscape,

> So suitable did this form [of telephone box] prove to the streets, countryside, and villages of England that it would often be seen on Christmas cards, upright in a sea of snow, beside the Gothic spire, the gabled cottage, and the five-barred gate. And it was a paradigm of what street architecture should be: permanent, dignified, and expressing an idea of public and legitimate order.
>
> With the privatization of the telephone network, Britain took a giant leap into the future.
>
> (Scruton 1996)

FIGURE 1.7 *Gilbert Scott,* Telephone Box, *1924. © Hawton telephone kiosk by Alan Murray-Rust, 2012.*

We might suppose that privatization *is* a conservative Utopian vision. Certainly, the 'giant leap' is Utopian in its prospective, rather than retrospective, conception of design. Scruton's defence of the telephone box is, therefore, clearly Arcadian in Auden's sense, and demonstrates the particular form of conservatism to which Scruton adheres.

Both Arcadians and Utopians are united in their efforts to move away from the present circumstances each finds disagreeable. (Hence Auden's Arcadian view of such circumstances as the result of our fall from grace.) But if Arcadians and Utopians are diametrically opposed, and if this opposition comes from a pre-rational sense of our feeling unease at our need to dwell, then we might expect to find the divisions between the two camps deeper than reason. How can art criticism, the place for reasoned aesthetic evaluation, survive these depths? We seem doomed to drown in the murky profundity of the Heideggerian abyss. The answer is to recognize the different attractions of the Arcadian and the Utopian, and to recognize that neither Arcadian nor Utopian has the single complete answer to our aesthetic needs. Each has, as it were, a position that requires reason-giving in its attempt to *persuade* us of its aesthetic worth.

Auden recognized this, as Jacobs observes in his introduction,

> Primarily through Rosetta's reminiscences, Auden clearly and powerfully presents the appeal of this Victorian Eden – but equally clearly and powerfully identifies it as a fantasy: not truly historical, and not a legitimate way of resolving 'our predicament.' ('[John] Betjeman is really a minor poet, of course,' he told [Alan] Ansen, and the judgment is rooted in Auden's perception that Betjeman failed to see that the world he so vividly imagined in his verse was, if partially real, also partly nostalgic fantasy.) (...) The Arcadian temptation is in the end just as deceptive as the Utopian one of the 'new barbarians.'
>
> (Jacobs 2011, xxiv–xxv)

It is not that they both fail. Rather, each has something to persuade us of it. Supported by reasons, each is, in its own terms, recommended.

Auden's diagnosis of the Fall is provided by allegory. The four have fallen into conversation and then, led by Rosetta's dreamlike musings, they consider the seven stages of the unconscious.

> Awakened at closing time, they join in a yearning lament for an archetypal father figure (…)
>
> The machinery of allegory in Auden's eclogue is derived, chiefly, from the psychological theories of C. G. Jung and from the existentialist philosophies of Heidegger, Jaspers and Kierkegaard, as well as from the main stream of Judeo-Christian belief. The chance encounter of the four strangers in a Third Avenue bar becomes, as psychological allegory, a manifestation of Jung's concept of the disintegration of the psyche into four differentiated functions: Thought (Malin), Feeling (Rosetta), Intuition (Quant), and Sensation (Emble). And the allegorical landscape explored by these personified functions is an inner landscape of the psyche encompassing the realms of the personal and collective unconsciousness. The superimposed spiritual allegory presupposes the disintegration of the faculties inherited from the Fall.
>
> (Callan 1965, 155–6)

Rosetta represents 'feeling', and, as such, this makes her a complex character. As Callan puts it, she 'usually expresses her feelings through an imagery of pleasant and unpleasant scenes' (Callan 1965, 156). Her character can be seen as an internal recognition of the distance she has fallen from the innocent world she craves, and the reckless life she pursues despite this desire. Later in the poem she refers to her father's house and to the path that would return her to her grandmother's, in each case identifying a building from which she is removed, respectively a symbol of her father's authority and a symbol of her innocence.

If Auden is an Arcadian, notwithstanding his criticism of Betjemen, then he is critical of modernity and this shows up in the sympathy with which he portrays Rosetta.

Scruton is also sceptical of the new Utopians, in whose number he includes Frank Ghery and Daniel Libeskind; Richard Rogers and Norman Foster. Each of his critical remarks upon architecture is either an excoriation of the modern (in which he includes the postmodern) or a retrospective defence of architectural heritage – most usually in the form of classicism.

However, he makes an effort to defend what Auden has called the Arcadians. His melancholia is evident even if his mood is ameliorated by the defence he offers. He embarks by removing his feet from the hard, intellectual grounds of scientific reason and then planting them on the softer lawns of our more general human outlook. In this he follows Kant, who had laboured to furnish both the practical and aesthetic aspects of our minds with a rational foundation. Theoretical reason, the subject of Kant's *Critique of Pure Reason*, examined the ways in which we warrant belief and sought to secure grounds for both our inductive and deductive forms of argument, each of which aims at the delivery of new truths. In his subsequent *Critique of Practical Reason*, he argued there are reasons that can compel us to act in certain ways, on pain of rationality, that do not take us to beliefs as conclusions. Given certain circumstances, I do not form a new belief. Rather, those circumstances alone provide reason to act.

Accepting a piece of practical reason is to act upon it. Aesthetic judgement is objective in a manner that, like practical reason, does not seek truth as its end. Rather, the conclusion of aesthetic reasoning is the acceptance of a recommendation to experience an object, scene or event, under a certain prescribed light. (This remains the case even if the prescription is self-produced; as when I choose to 'see' a work under a certain description that provides, thereby, an advantageous experience.) It is true of both art and nature, each of which affords aesthetic experience. It is the job of the critic (including the self-as-critic) to arrive at these recommendations which emerge as judgements. Such judgements are both subjective (in that they are essentially experiential, and there can be no experience that is not endured by some particular subject) and universal (in that they are recommended by reason as both pleasurable, intelligible and, through their intelligibility, can be shared amongst us). Simon Blackburn puts this clearly,

> For Kant, concerned with the judgement of taste, the salient problem was how there *could be* such a judgement, when aesthetics had to do more with felt pleasure than with applying a concept according to a rule.
>
> (Blackburn 1998, 111)

Felt pleasures are subjective. Kant's great work in aesthetics provides us with an account of how it is we can feel such pleasures are justified. Hence, in appreciating art, we do not proceed along arguments that carry us towards truth; nor do we conduct our reflections in order to arrive at a course of action required. We enjoy aesthetic pleasures and do so as a practice in which we are rationally engaged and in which we exercise reasoned judgement.

IX The application of reasoned judgement

To get a flavour of such judgements as they pertain to architecture, we can turn to the novel by Antonio Muñoz Molina, *In the Night of Time* (Muñoz Molina 2015). The novel's central fictional character Ignacio Abel is an architect who is designing University City on the outskirts of Madrid at the outbreak of the Spanish Civil War. Abel, our architect, is working on the School of Philosophy and Letters,

> [Abel] liked that moment of stillness at the end of the day; the deep stillness of places where people have worked hard, the silence that follows the rumble and vibrations of machinery, the ringing of telephones, the shouts of men; the solitude of a place where a crowd rushed through seconds before, people busy with tasks, fulfilling their duties, doing their part in the general undertaking. The son of a construction foreman, accustomed since childhood to dealing with masons and working with his hands, Ignacio Abel maintained a practical, sentimental affection for the specific trade skills that were transformed into the character traits of the men who cultivated them. The draftsman who inked a right angle on a plan, the bricklayer who spread a base of fresh mortar and smoothed it with the trowel before placing the brick on top of it, the woodworker who sanded the curve of a banister, the glazier who cut the exact dimensions of the pane of glass for a window, the master craftsman who verified with a plumb line the veracity of a wall, the stonecutter who cut a paving stone or the stone block for a curb or the plinth of a column.
>
> (Muñoz Molina 2015, 27)

These three sentences have a protracted incantatory character, as does much of Muñoz Molina's writing. But the quotidian bits and pieces that contribute to the construction of the building begin to take on a more remarkable aspect as the smallest detail comes into focus. We imagine the master craftsman with his plumb line checking – probably without need – the veracity of the wall. This passage gets us to think of the making of the building as a process of coöperative work. In this we catch the whiff of socialism, the coming together of a community of makers, each furthering the project with their individually accumulated and their together aggregated skills.

The film, *Witness*, has a federal agent protecting a female witness. She is an Amish woman and during the agent's assignment he immerses himself in the Amish community to which she belongs. There is one scene where the community come together to build a barn in a day – by hand. It is an extraordinary event and it symbolizes what it is that we do as members of a larger body: the collective.

A factual example might illustrate the point. The Royal Festival Hall (RFH), designed in 1948 as an integral part of the Festival of Britain, is a concert hall on London's South Bank. The festival was a celebration of postwar optimism and the RFH was its flagship building, designed by a team of architects who taught in the architecture schools. The team was assembled by the London County Council. The team included the young designer and author, Trevor Dannatt,

> Dannatt detailed the staircases and glazed screens of the foyers, along with some of the external windows and last minute furnishings. He explained how each balustrade has a notch running up its centre for one's thumbs; how the main foyer stopped short of the riverfront for a double-height restaurant with its own spiral stair; that the columns on the main floor were lined with timber and how each element has a flash gap, creating a shadow that defined and separated it from the rest.
>
> (Harwood 2021)

Dannatt's sensitivity to the shadow is something critics of modernism omit. The notch for the thumb on the balustrade shows him to be a designer in the cast of Muñoz Molina's Abel. Muñoz Molina mentions the inked right-angle on the drawing paper but goes on to detail the work of Abel, the designer,

> Now his hands were too delicate and couldn't have endured the roughness of the materials, and they never had acquired the wisdom

> of touch he'd observed as a boy in his father and the men who worked with him. His fingers brushed soft Bristol board and paper, handled rulers, compasses, drawing pencils, water colour brushes, moved quickly on a typewriter, skillfully dialed phone numbers, closed around the curved black lacquer of his fountain pen as he inked signatures on paperwork. But somewhere he'd kept the memory that longed for the feel of tools and objects in his hands.
> (Muñoz Molina 2015)

We could now think of each contributor to the achievement of the School of Philosophy and Letters building at University City, as hefted to his task; and this further description of Abel is to point out that the architect is also hefted to the tools of his trade and by extension to the feeling for material that his proximity to the actual construction affords him.

Abel, the fictional architect of University City is based on one of its actual architects, Agustín Aguirre López. Republican politician Juan Negrín saved the fictional architect from execution at University City in Muñoz Molina's novel. In fact, 'Negrín saved the architect Agustín Aguirre from ending up in an anonymous grave in the Casa de Campo or in the University City itself' (Muñoz Molina 2009). The architecture of the University becomes symbolic in the novel and in his newspaper essay Muñoz Molina presages his fictional account in his review of an exhibition entitled, 'Un edificio, un símbolo' ('A building, a symbol'), in the Spanish national daily paper, *El Pais*. It is here he writes of the building's significance, combining a political interpretation with an aesthetic appraisal,

> [O]n January 15, 1933, President Alcalá-Zamora and the highest authorities of the Republic inaugurated the first faculty of the University City, still under construction for the most part. Other buildings have been designed in the dusty historicist styles that are still cultivated at the time: Philosophy, designed by the young architect Agustín Aguirre, is a fully modern work, with spacious interior spaces and large windows, with a terrace that overlooks the Sierra de Guadarrama. Every detail has been thought to fit its function and to reveal it brilliantly; The architect has also designed the benches, the classroom signs, the study tables, the furniture in the dining room bar, in which there is an unusual innovation in Spain, a self-service. Agustín Aguirre has worked in a continuous and fertile dialogue with the dean of the faculty,

> Manuel García Morente, for whom the shape of the building expresses his own intellectual and educational ambitions: the university has to get out of the physical claustrophobia of the old classrooms in mansions dark and also of a sclerotic teaching anchored in the monologues of the professors and in the routine of the tests learned by heart.

He goes on,

> Agustín Aguirre invents a building that favors both recollection and expansion, with bright classrooms and a forklift to load the library's books faster, with an interior clarity that is that of rigorous and pleasant study and that of what Juan Ramón Jiménez called the museum of windows: the possibility of raising your eyes from the book and looking out the window at the spectacle of common life and nature.

Of the exhibition he is reviewing, Muñoz Molina continues,

> Some of these things we can still touch: the modern shape of the benches, their wood that the years darkened, the curvature of the arm of an armchair, the leather of its back. With the emotion of the most fragile objects that bear witness to time because they were saved from it, we touch the smooth surface of a blackboard or the brittle rubber of a map, or we see behind the glass of a display case the leaves of a manuscript by [José Ortega y Gasset], a notebook of the notes that a student took in Pedro Salinas's literature class, the photo of a passport with the crenellated seal of the Spanish Republic, an exam paper. The closeness between things restores links that were extinguished in the distant past: in a glass case there is a typewritten copy of the thesis of an American student, Katherine Whitmore; a little further on is the first edition of *La voz a ti dueda*, [*My Voice Because of You*] with the poems secretly dedicated to Whitmore by Professor Salinas. The students all wear suits and ties, comb their hair in a straight [parting], often have round glasses; the girls, small and smiling, are innumerable. In an essay included in the catalogue, José Gaos acutely observes that the presence of women in the faculty instinctively civilized the men.
>
> (Muñoz Molina 2009)

Returning to the novel, another passage internalizes the conflict we have already noted between the Arcadians and the Utopians. Abel studied at the Bauhaus and whilst we have noted that he was sensitized to the work of the builder by his father and his co-workers, his acquaintance with modernism and its laudable ambitions gets an airing. Abel is capable of entertaining two seemingly contradictory perspectives upon architecture and the form it should take. The subjective aspect of aesthetic experience is adverted to in these two passages, each of which nevertheless provides reasons for taking architecture in a certain way. The first comes as Abel considers his younger acceptance of modernism of which he now has misgivings,

> The anonymous masters of architecture had worked with what they had closest to hand, not with materials they'd selected but with those provided by chance, stone or wood or clay for adobe bricks.
>
> (Muñoz Molina 2015, 184)

(Note the 'closest to hand' that recalls Heidegger, and also the classicists' representation of the origins of building as that is to be found in the base/ column/ capital/ beam configuration of mythical Ur-vernacular construction) He continues,

> In 1929 he'd travelled to Barcelona expressly to see the German pavilion at the International Exposition, and as he studied with [his professor] the rooms of marble and steel and glass walls, he'd discovered in himself, beneath the admiration, an element of rejection. The perfection that only a few years earlier would have seemed indisputable disturbed him now for its coldness, over which it seemed the human presence would slide without leaving a trace.
>
> (Muñoz Molina 2015, 184–5)

Muñoz Molina constructs Abel's reflection in such a way that the character is able to 'love' the materials and the uses to which they are put in Mies van der Rohe's pavilion. It's just that they do not contain the human touches whose absence disturbs our protagonist. Much later in the book, he again considers the pavilion. (Abel's father was a foreman and a stonemason in the fiction. Mies' father was a

FIGURE 1.8 *Mies van der Rohe, German Pavilion, Barcelona International Exposition, 1929 (reconstructed 1983–6) © Ashley Pomeroy at English Wikipedia, 2010.*

stonemason in fact.) Now exiled in America, Abel is commissioned to design a college library,

> He understands that the sketches [preliminary designs] he's made are useless. The building can't have existed in his imagination with that diamond-like perfection he's admired in Mies van der Rohe's pavilion in Barcelona.
>
> (Muñoz Molina 2015, 537)

Abel's fear, born of his humanism, is that the pavilion manifests a 'coldness, over which it seemed the human presence would slide without leaving a trace'. However, we could argue that we launder our clothes to remove the odour secreted into them by our routine efforts; mop our kitchens, polish the cutlery, vacuum the carpets, dust the pelmets, scrub our doorsteps, clean the windows, and all of this is precisely to erase the trace of human *being*. Or else we might descend into squalor.

Ed Kienholz, the American sculptor, once remarked that to really understand a culture you should visit its flea-markets, its stalls scattered with upturned boxes of house clearance bric-a-brac, the collected effects of the recently dead; the accumulated private and personal memorabilia of lives now completed; the photograph albums with their black-and-white images of loved friends and family; of secret lovers and prouder moments of sporting prowess; of beloved cats and dogs; Eiffel's tower and other places of interest: the night we drank absinthe in Chez Georges. What was once ready-to-hand becomes present-at-hand, when ruined, broken or abandoned. The flea-market dumps the possessions of the dead across its stalls. Artists like Kienholz or Joseph Cornell engage in a rescue mission – not to make these objects ready-to-hand once more. Rather, to raise them up into sacred memories: things in themselves; good-for-nothings; works of contemplative pleasure: art.

The impetus to make architecture arises from the residue of the lives we lead or the lives that others have led. Must everything bear

FIGURE 1.9 *Ed and Nancy Kienholz,* Lavapies: Drawing for Commercial *#2, 1973, assemblage. © Fred Romero, 2017.*

the stain of human passage – bearing witness to its collapse? Must architecture either gleam or be tarnished in order to lend itself to the accommodation of our lives?

Abel internalizes the aesthetic argument, it is framed as a personal conflict; but the two positions manifest a real dilemma in our judgements concerning works of art. The arguments need not be internal, but so seen, they defy resolution. Can one not see the point of the music of Richard Wagner – really grasp what he wanted to do with respect to tradition – whilst at the same time appreciating Erik Satie's measured response? It is the privilege of the spectator, after all, to remain aloof from artistic confrontations born of aesthetic commitments. (It is, perhaps, the burden of the artist that she must take an artistic stance, and that burden runs the risk of weighing heavily upon her aesthetic choices.)

The separation of the artist's role from that of the spectator does not support relativism. As we noted above, to accept as reason for a particular valuable aesthetic experience some persuasive suggestion does not require that we arrive at a new belief. It means that we undergo an experience of the kind recommended. We can take pleasure in both Wagner and Satie, and we can have independent good reasons for engaging with each.

The artist, however, in her commitment to an aesthetic ideal, may have to forgo the pleasure afforded by another work if the artistic commitment of that other work's creator is opposed to hers. It is possible Satie did not, because he could not, given his artistic commitments, permit himself to hear the beauty in Wagner's *Tristan und Isolde*. However, even if this is generally the case, it remains merely contingent. The spectator and the artist are two roles the artist can, perhaps psychologically she must, adopt. So that in making the work of art she submits to the regulative perspective of the spectator. And so, the internalization of the two points of view, accredited to Abel by Muñoz Molina, helps us to see how these two aesthetic responses might arise in one and the same breast. Why *must* the apparent conflict foreclose the availability of spectator *and* artist occupying the view from no-man's-land?

It is perfectly coherent, on this view, that Abel should be persuaded of the beauty of the German pavilion, because it uses modern materials that open up the building in ways in which classical, Romanesque, byzantine or vernacular architecture could not. The materials thus exploited, in the comfortable climate of Catalonia, need no barrier between inside and out; and thus, modernist architecture's 'transparency' is opened up to the elements in ways that concerns over shelter and security would inhibit. Of course, the pavilion was part of a world fair; and to that end Mies was demonstrating what a building – a truly modern building – could be like.

Simultaneously, Abel could be persuaded by the beauty of the Cathedral of the Holy Cross and St. Eulalia in Barcelona, with its shaded cloister and its worn flagstones, the forensic attention to which he could trace the route from the refectory to the chapel, along with many other palimpsestic observations of a monastic life no longer pursued.

FIGURE 1.10 Cathedral of Saint Eulalia and the Holy Cross, *Cloister, Barcelona © José Luis Filpo Cabana, 2012.*

In each case he would be able to say, 'Look at this', and, pointing in turn at each building, he could add either, 'How bright and filled with light, almost as if light were a stuff made of fresh air that circulates within the small jewel like edifice'; or, 'Think of their lives as the monks processed from the modest meal, returning to their considerations of the world and their place in it, and how they would have looked on with pleasure at the thirteen geese that live in the enclosed cloistered garden. Part of the beauty,' he would continue, 'is that we follow on the same worn path as the monks; and we look upon the geese as symbols of the thirteen years Saint Eulalia lived until her martyrdom. We look at the architectural details with the same eyes as did those monks who noticed the way the light falls and the shadows form in the cloisters; and the brightness of the Mediterranean light that would shortly give way to the dark cool interior of the cathedral and the quiet calmness of prayer. The smells are the same for us as for them; our experience now, shaped by theirs.' And then: 'How clean the lines; and how that in turn brings us to consider the pattern of the marble, its revelation of its ancient past, the stone, itself the stuff of the petrified cosmos, disclosing the strata of millennia in its surface pattern; and the glass, a silicate of sand and dating back to 1400 B.C.E.; a clear and magical stuff, bequeathed to us from Mesopotamia and here in its modernity and in such expanses as the Mesopotamians would not have imagined.'

Back to the cathedral. Prayer and other forms of devotion are not optional for the monks who may, nevertheless, experience doubt as part of their faith. How then do we respond to this cathedral? For those of us for whom secular modernity has replaced religious sentiment, prayer and other forms of devotion are not options. It would be inauthentic. We cannot, therefore, inhabit the cathedral in the ways in which the monks once did. We cannot pretend to believe in the death and resurrection, but we can entertain the value of religious life with respect for the commitment of those who follow in faith. We can, as it were, experience the cathedral from a distance.

Abel, therefore, can appreciate the symbolism of the cathedral with its time-worn steps and the dim and dusty niches and he can value it through the aesthetic experience it affords. So too, can he appreciate the fresh, 'cleaned-out' modernism of the German pavilion, with its untarnished 'newness' and its optimistic Utopian air. He can appreciate both and his enjoyment of each will be supported by aesthetic considerations which rise to the level of reason when the appropriate experience is undertaken.

This is, surely, what Kant – in his great scheme, surveying the human mind – had to tell us. In particular his work invites us to think: that if architecture is an art that accommodates us, then we occupy a certain sort of life in which the building plays a constitutional part. However, when we make aesthetic judgements about that life and the building's part in it, we can make judgements about the kind of value the building has for us, and then critics can further flesh out the detail of that value for specific works by pulling detail into focus. 'See it like this.'

X Reasons to believe and reasons to act

The distinction between reasons to believe, aiming at truth, and reasons to act, aiming at goodness, provides scope for thinking in terms of human flourishing under two aspects. The first is intellectual, the second is moral. The first kind of reason is independent of our peculiar human perspective. In arriving at our conclusions, we will find ourselves assessing the world as an independent state of affairs. The second kind of reason aims at action. It is guided by wisdom, rather than truth. Reasons to act belong in the human world and they are restricted by human concerns. That is not true of the non-perspectival scientific view.

We can, and perhaps should, live as if we are dignified by our place in creation, notwithstanding the harsher truths of 'the view from nowhere'. For we do not, and perhaps we cannot, occupy the view from nowhere. The scientific point of view is, in this sense, uninhabitable. Our lives and our leading of them are necessarily perspectival – they have an unavoidable subjective element. In celebration and in grief we see the world from a point of view that is ours alone. The tiny, sub-atomic particles, for which the scientists search, cast no light upon the movement of the human soul. Italian philosophers Roberto Casati and Achille C. Varzi put this rather nicely,

> There is physical structure on the scale of millimicrons at one extreme and on the scale of light years at another. But surely the appropriate scale for animals is the intermediate one of

> millimeters to kilometers, and it is appropriate because the world and the animal are then comparable.
>
> (Casati and Varzi 1999, 73)

It is our embeddedness *as animals* that constricts our view out onto the world. We are animals unable to gaze upon the world from anywhere but our own perspective. We are humans too; and human animals are both fettered by, and liberated by, reason. We engage with the world as that is made up of middle-sized objects, roughly the 'intermediate one', of which Casati and Varzi write. It was in the context of Kant's constraint upon the exercise of reason that it should be always employed within the framework of experience, that we saw the importance of the middle-sized. The human world just is the world as experienced.

Thus, we are concerned in aesthetics with the human world and our condition in and of that world. Scruton, as we have seen, dances at the same end of the ballroom and to the same tune as the continental philosophers who seek to understand what it is to be human – by and large: the phenomenologists. In the opening pages of her delightful book, *At the Existentialist Café*, Sarah Bakewell tells us of a meeting in Paris, at the Bec-de-Gaz bar in Montparnasse, between Beauvoir, Sartre and Raymond Aron. (Aron had been studying in Berlin.) The three were drinking the house speciality, apricot cocktails. It was Aron who told the other two about the new philosophy and 'he recommended the phenomenological method: disregard intellectual clutter, pay attention to things and let them reveal themselves to you.'

> 'you see, *mon petit camarade*,' said Aron to Sartre – 'my little comrade', his pet name for him since their schooldays – 'if you are a phenomenologist, you can talk about this cocktail and make philosophy out of it'
>
> Beauvoir wrote that Sartre turned pale on hearing this. She made it sound more dramatic by implying that they had never heard of phenomenology at all.
>
> (Bakewell 2016, 3)

(For anyone tempted, I have found two recipes for such an apricot cocktail but neither makes reference to Paris. One is 'the Claridge'. The other has the addition of vermouth and is called 'Claridge's cocktail.') (Complete Cocktails 2013, 40)

How do things reveal themselves to us? Look! And keep looking. The looking is not merely turning our perceptual apparatus on and allowing the sensations to flood in. Rather, in looking we attend to things and think through them. Observation and attention are modes of getting to know the world, and thereby letting it reveal itself to us. Think again of Jane Bustin's *Tablet ii* (2014). What we need to take from this is that appearances are important – *all-important* – in our efforts to understand aesthetic experience as that is encountered in the visual arts. For, as we have noted, such experience is both sensual and thoughtful. This is what grounds Scruton's dismissal of much art theory as scientism. It is appearance that matters most in aesthetics, and we have to be prepared for them.

> Perhaps Scruton would have been horrified to be discussed under the heading 'Phenomenology'. I discuss him under this label because his approach is (...) focused on the experience of buildings. (...) In particular, he emphasises the freedom of the imagination of the *observer* rather than that of the architect, the client, the inhabitant, or other users of the building.
>
> (Guyer 2021, 118)

Guyer, I believe, is right to bring Scruton under the broad umbrella of phenomenology, despite Wittgenstein having remarked, 'There is no such thing as phenomenology, but there are indeed phenomenological problems' (Wittgenstein 2007, §53). Wittgenstein rejected the phenomenologists' philosophy of mind regarding the priority of the first-person point of view. Scruton would half agree. He regards phenomenology as having two ambitions. The first is to provide a description of the *Lebenswelt*, the second is to adopt a system whereby the subject is central. Scruton takes up the first task and it is pursued throughout his work. In so doing, he writes in complaint against analytical philosophy, for its incompetence 'either to discuss the complexities of individual experience, or to resolve the "phenomenological problems" which are generated by the attempt to describe it' (Scruton 2006, Appendix 1). His broad approach to philosophy, and his perspective upon its importance, takes seriously this need to place the human being in a world she understands and in which she feels at home. The kind of understanding here sought is that in which a subject is able to interact with her socially constructed environment.

Scruton, following Wittgenstein, recognized the priority of appearance in some philosophical matters. For the time being we should note that the Wittgenstein quote above comes from his *Remarks on Colour*, and that it contains a warning.

Here is Scruton in conversation with Karsten Harries, as transcribed in *Architecture Philosophy* by Tom Spector. The discussion has turned to Heidegger's 'Building Dwelling Thinking':

> Scruton: I think the word '*wohnen*,' which is in the title of Heidegger's essay, could also be translated as 'settlement.' I think that's really what he had in mind, and that's something that all humans need. We are, naturally, settled beings (…)
> Harries: I am surprised to hear you quoting Heidegger!
> Scruton: I am an educated man! [Laughs]
>
> (Harries et al. 2017)

Elsewhere, Scruton writes of the hearth,

> In the religion of the ancient Greeks and Romans the hearth, and the fire that glows in it, have a special significance, as representing the will to settle of the family whose land lies round about. It is here that room is made for the household gods, and it is here that members of the family gather for the ritual acknowledgement of the ancestors who established their title to be where they are (…) The Vedas [the large body of ancient Indian religious Sanskrit text] make much of *Agni*, the god of fire (Latin *ignus*), who sanctifies the hearth, and protects it as the sovereign sphere of the family that eats, prays, and rests in its vicinity.
>
> (Scruton 2014, 118)

For Scruton, the grander the symbol of our historic status as a people, the more hopeless the tragedy of our fall from grace. And so *we*, this squalor, this litter of imperfection writ large, must seek atonement in antiquity. *In the name of the Father, etcetera.*

Hence the mythical promise of a return home to the temple, the classical design of which was handed down on stone tablets to Moses on Mount Sinai. Quinlan Terry, the contemporary British architect, goes so far as to aver the truth of this myth. If correct, he has God on his side. Terry's is an eccentric position, even amongst classicists. Scruton talks of the tablet as handed down by Moses but makes no claim for the literal truth of the episode described. If Terry is right, though, we must suppose that under God's prescription, recorded in Mosaic Law, it is imperative we pursue the classical tradition. That's an awfully big 'If'. Scruton goes only so far in his mythologizing, stopping short of metaphysical realism with respect to his engagement with scripture.

Against such myth-making, Richard Wollheim writes in the first paragraph of his William James Lectures given in 1982 and later published as *The Thread of Life*,

> Lots of things which aren't even living have lives, such as alpha-particles, or refrigerators, or the great city of Venice, and of those things which have lives and are living, many don't lead their lives, such as oak trees, or the saints in heaven, or domesticated animals.
>
> (Wollheim 1984, 1)

Why, apart from his irrepressible mischief, would he focus on 'the saints in heaven'? The saints cannot lead their lives because they have already been led and judged supererogatory. How can they now act in heaven? What could they do? Even if they cannot act, for what could they hope or of what could they despair? And, if it makes no sense to ask how they could lead their lives, then how could they live?

There is an incoherence in the idea of heaven, where 'dwell' the saints. For they cannot dwell in the manner of our occupation of the world. And so, it is, even as a myth, an incoherent narrative.

Scruton, then, should have to say something about the, at least apparent, incoherence of heaven and earth and the lives of those who dwell in each sphere. It rather looks as if heaven is empty, and that is scant consolation for the communion of souls to which he hopes to belong, in whatever way that is possible. (Others among us may find solace in what we take to be the correlative view that hell is also empty. Difficult to tell whether the two claims are supposed to be necessary truths or contingent. If necessary, it is hard to see the point of using them as reward and punishment respectively. But, if contingent, the first offers only the slightest hope of redemption from sin, whilst the second is chilling. Imagine becoming the first and only eternal occupant of hell!)

Yet thoughts of the sacred, mythical as they might be, serve to ground the conservatism of Roger Scruton, and through that conservatism (miniscule 'c') he derives his Conservatism (majuscule 'C'). There is much to admire in Scruton's aesthetics but we need not agree with his anti-modernist aesthetic, or at least those parts of it that lead us back to the scripture of classicism. His defence of the *Lebenswelt* is secured independently of any such sacred meaning.

To see the place that Scruton assigns to myth, and to think of that place as the foundation of his idea of culture, we might look at the last page of his *The Soul of the World*, where he writes,

> The afterlife as a condition that succeeds death in time, is an absurdity. For succession in time belongs within the causal envelope, in the space-time continuum that is the world of nature. If there is any message to be extracted from my arguments, it is that the idea of salvation – of a right relation to the creator – in no way requires eternal life, so conceived (…) Religion, as I have been considering it, does not describe the natural world but the *Lebenswelt*, the world of subjects, using allegories and myths in order to remind us at the deepest level of who and what we are. (Scruton 2014, 198)

Even granting Scruton's delicate reasoning concerning the place of the subject in the world and her need to find a home within it, we might find his conclusions too conservative – unrelenting in their rejection of modernism. Couldn't modernism be equally conceived as the kind of home that, at least in the abstract, moves forward in accordance with our better understanding of our natural place in the world. Couldn't new techniques be seen as presenting new opportunities for us to exploit our occupation of the world, and our settlement within it?

To be sure, Scruton, consistent with his endorsement of electric lighting that imitates gas lighting, regards pressed tin classical detail adorning twentieth-century New York warehouses as permissible, even laudable. However, that is a preference for an architectural aesthetic that hides its exploitation of new materials rather than finds ways in which to take advantage of aesthetic opportunities. The pressed tin detail merely apes its predecessor, rather than explores an aesthetic opportunity provided by some new technique. The tin detail uses new techniques merely to keep faith with traditional design. The aesthetic exploitation of new techniques affords new experiences within the art of architecture, the former constrains and inhibits, the latter liberates and licences change. Cannot expansive glass sheets bring light into the hovel?

A more liberal view of modernism, embracing its continuity with tradition, is set out by Wollheim in consideration of painting,

> Within the concept of art under which most of the finest, certainly most of the boldest, works of our age have been made, the connotation of physicality moves to the fore.
>
> The evidence for such a theory at work is manifold, the inspiration of the theory can be seen in a wide variety of phenomena which it thereby unifies [for instance]: (...) the physical juxtaposition of disparate or borrowed elements, sometimes stuck on, sometimes freestanding, to the central body of the work, as in collage or assemblages.
>
> (Wollheim 1973, 118)

Modernist practices make available all manner of stuffs for recruitment to the activity of painting. These can include, amongst other things, photography, three-dimensional elements, text, fabric and printed material. Whilst collage has been around for a long time, its use in modernism marks it out as a radical technique of making images. (The National Galleries of Scotland mounted an exhibition, *Cut and Paste: 400 Years of Collage* in 2019.)

It seems absurd to proscribe its use in fine art. It seems equally absurd to prohibit modern techniques in architecture – the use of structural glass, the spanning of spaces with structural rolled steel joists, the use of heightened tiers of accommodation (skyscrapers) permitted by engineering development and so on. These new techniques across the arts provide opportunities for us to express anew our situation – a situation which is, itself, new.

However, as noted above, it is at the juncture of psychology, anthropology and philosophy that aesthetics gets its warrant. For it is within the strictures of these disciplines that we come to understand ourselves as human beings. The fine arts can help us grasp these matters by providing experiences that get us to *apprehend*, to *appreciate* and to *accept* our situation; to take it into our embrace.

Scruton's philosophical view does not seek mythology as the true historical account. Rather, he seeks to give the ground under which we might view mythology. Scruton gives philosophical grounds for accepting mythology, not as a statement of fact, but as a 'given' way of life – one that we inherit without the kind of question that arises from taking a scientific view. If this is our given way of life, he claims, we should accept it. He therefore disables the 'scientific' question, 'Is it true?', replacing it with the livelier question, 'Is this how we should live?', which admits of no truth but is answered with a recommendation.

Scruton goes further, thinking that we can have inherent needs, one of which is, at least something like, dwelling. And to this he adds a religious dimension, offering the sacred as a dimension in which we must live if we are to fulfil our potential as rational beings. Scruton comments,

> In a brief fit of lucidity Heidegger wrote that it is only by dwelling that we build: building and dwelling are parts of a single enterprise, whereby we hunter-gatherers overcome our nature and begin the work of civilization, which has the temple, the market and the city as its goals.
>
> (Scruton 2005, 206)

Further on he contrasts the visions of Matthew Arnold and Friedrich Nietzsche,

> The distinction between Arnold and Nietzsche is the distinction between two kinds of loss. Arnold's loss of faith occurs in a world made by faith, in which all the outer trappings of a religious community remain in place, like the outward signs of holiness in a Gothic Revival church. Nietzsche's loss of faith is an absolute loss, a loss not only of inward conviction but of the outward symbols that make it possible. (…) Loss of faith for Arnold is a personal tragedy, to be mourned but concealed. Loss of faith for Nietzsche is an existential transfiguration, to be accepted and affirmed, since the world no longer permits an alternative.
>
> (Scruton 2005, 220)

We are now returned to something like Auden's distinction between Arcadians and Utopians. However, we have seen how our conception of what we are is intimately bound up with our notion of dwelling. If architecture is an art, it is necessary to demonstrate how its materials are fashioned into a medium such that we both enjoy and appreciate its works.

XI The Apollonian and the Dionysian

Scruton is not alone. Gordon Graham sets a challenge for the arts (Graham 2007). How can the arts, in their present secularized manifestation, help us to re-enchant the world? The Arcadian world was regulated temporally by the seasons and by the festivities that marked out the beginnings and/or the culminations of those festivities. Christianity, Judaism, Islam, Hinduism, Buddhism, Sikhism, Shinto, Zoroastrianism and other faiths, all have calendars for the year during which we congregate on feast days and at celebrations of rites of passage. Attached to many of these celebrations are various special devotions, calling upon the faithful to affirm their faith and to recognize their communion in the rite observed. Such celebration might include music, dance, acting, all to be carried out in places decked out in traditional decoration, perhaps with images to remind the faithful of the miraculous events pertaining to the particular religion in which their activities are made sacred.

It is easy to see why there might be a special place upon which such things as altars are built; and for many, if not all, there are festivals in which communion with the dead is central to the celebration. And so, special places, temples, become the place of communion with fellow believers, and in the temple various rituals unfold among the specially decorated setting for this feast.

Graham identifies the feast, and the work of art within the celebration of the feast, with the Dionysian conception of *lived* art. Music is such an art in that its rehearsal is a contribution to, and a constituent element of, the ritual of the Holy Mass, for instance. The paintings of the stations of the cross in Roman Catholic churches are part of a ritual passage during which the faithful remember Christ's passion. So thinking, these arts sanctify music, painting, wine and bread. The burning of incense during oblation changes the space in which the worshipers stand or kneel in prayer.

Graham calls upon the distinction articulated by Nietzsche between this Dionysian conception of art and the Apollonian perspective, between what Nietzsche identified respectively as intoxication and dream. It is with intoxication that we engage in ritual. For Graham, if not for Nietzche, the Apollonian is identified with Kant's formalism.

Graham writes of the enchantment of such occasions and places that enchantment (the casting of a spell in lyric or song) at the centre of a community's coming together as a body, in prayer for rain or in celebration of the harvest; or on a day devoted to a saint or god; or to express gratitude for nature's bounty, to celebrate a wedding, a birth, or a life now completed. And so, the temple, with its altar, is the focus of the community and the communion which it celebrates, and it is art in its various forms that decorate the temple and adjust its space to the particular feast under observation. Graham thinks of post-enlightenment art as having fled the holy precincts of the temple and come to live and be loved in a void that no longer serves the community as a binding force. Art no longer ministers to our religious yearning. His challenge is for contemporary artists to redirect their work in order to re-enchant the world; to bring art back into the fold. If it is now impossible to mythologize our lives, at least art might bring consolation to our deprivation.

It is certainly true, as we shall see, that Kant's view of art is that it is, in the first place, the product of genius; and so it is for the artist who has risen above the norms of his merely talented contemporaries, whose work will stand the test of time; serving, as it will, as an example by which those contemporaries can make work themselves, even as that work will lack the originality required to achieve the status of genius. Thus, the art of the commune will lack genius and will, by Kantian standards, fall short of being *great* art.

If architecture is a fine art, on Kant's account, it must be shown to admit of genius and it must exhibit such genius by providing us with access to aesthetic ideas. The notion of an aesthetic idea in relation to the fine arts, broadly, will be undertaken in Chapter 5. In filling out that account we are to consider what pleasures a human being might enjoy, specifically those afforded by the arts; and how that pleasure can be expressed in judgements formed by aesthetic engagement, itself a manifestation of our rationality. The contribution of aesthetic ideas to our understanding of the medium of architecture will be dealt with in Chapter 7.

Returning to Scruton: he claims that architecture, being a public art, does not require genius. Indeed, he thinks that what we need are pattern books that can guide the practised builder in his construction of buildings fit for the environment of a settled community. If architecture is to be considered a fine art, that cannot be so. Therefore, we shall need to draw upon other resources to fund our claim that architecture is a fine art. This shall be the focus of Chapters 3 and 4.

Recent work has resurrected the notion that the fine arts are a collection of practices, each with its own set of constitutive rules. Arguably, painting is a representational art in which a two-dimensional plane is used to depict objects, scenes or events in which we can look to search for meaning. Poetry is a structured way of using language along with rules of composition that permit the form of the poem to exert its structure over a content that structure helps to express – or in some other way renders that content pertinent; it provides thought in a structured way that makes that thought immediately enlightening, as if that thought has occurred to us for the first time, whether it has or not. It is incumbent upon us, therefore, to find the manner in which architecture embodies such a medium, through which aesthetic response is made appropriate.

The conversation has circled, as conversations frequently do, though the circle in this case is not vicious. We have considered two different paths along which a theory of architecture might proceed. Indeed, we have looked and shall look again to see if there is reason to consider the confluence of these two paths. Our notion of dwelling informs the conception we have of who and what we are. Scruton stops short of metaphysical commitments to the ensoulment that Heidegger sought in his commitment to *being*. Nevertheless, Scruton sees, in architecture as elsewhere, a sacred dimension, and sees the importance of architecture in its accordance with that vision.

If, however, architecture is a fine art, then it is freed from the shackles that such an historicist view would place it within. That's another big 'if'. Let's see.

2

Home in the world

I War and Peace 2

In this chapter, we shall look at a number of cases of our trying to find our accommodation in the world. That enterprise has its roots in an attitude. We shall look at four different examples of 'homing' ourselves and see that the attitude engaged is strikingly the same across cultures and across the centuries. This 'architectural attitude' is projected onto the world, so that the world, *as we find it*, is appropriated to our projection. The attitude, as it were, is at the heart of what it is to think architecturally.

Home in the World is the title of Amartya Sen's memoir – of growing up in Santiniketan at his grandparents' house and studying as a boy at Rabindranath Tagore's school. It is from there he ventured forth to find home in the world. It is a striking account of the formation of not only the intellect but also the world view of the distinguished Nobel laureate (Economics) and former Master of Trinity College Cambridge. I use the title of his book as my chapter title with reverence. It is, after all, the very thing we are looking for; if not the 'how', then at least the 'what it is' to find home in the world. As previously mentioned, in order to seek out our identity, to establish *who we are,* to get a view of what we should count as *home*, we need to think of what it is for *us,* whomsoever we may be, to flourish.

The unity of the *sensus communis*, upon which Kant relies, has to take account of all those whose minds are structured along the lines Kant sets out. It may be that the only creatures to have minds are persons. Persons are to include not only humanity as a whole, but also international institutions, nations, companies,

God (and His choir of angels in heaven), other animals if ever they should develop minds – indeed any identifiable body to whom or to which we can attribute reason. (Excluded from personhood is anything that is incapable, in principle, of submitting thought to reason.) However extended our list of persons may become, we can, for our purposes, restrict our purview to human beings. Thus, we find in Kant, the grounds for much, if not all, our liberal views upon both the right forms of *theoretical reason* in general, and in particular, the *practical reason* establishing the human rights and duties of any man on account of his ability to reason and his consequent power to act upon it. (I use the term 'man' neutrally between sexual distinctions; and, therefore, it is for my purposes, genderless. I leave it to others to decide if this is an accurate interpretation of Kant's thought.) Persons, then, in virtue of their innate power of reason, are constituents of Kant's *sensus communis*.

Extending the *sensus sommunis* into the area of aesthetics, Kant, as we have seen, seeks to secure the rational basis upon which our judgements rest; to put it rather awkwardly: to judge at least some *experiences* in the light of reason. Our present, special interest within aesthetics lies within his remarks on the fine arts. We shall come to that in part two. For now, we are concerned with the wide sweep of his philosophy, resting, as it does, on his conception of freedom and reason.

We saw, in Chapter 1, the description Muñoz Molina provides in his review of the Philosophy building, at University City in Madrid, designed by the young architect Agustín Aguirre. The classroom with large windows and a terrace looked out over the Sierra de Guadarrama. '[W]hat Juan Ramón Jiménez called the museum of windows: the possibility of raising your eyes from the book and looking out the window at the spectacle of common life and nature.' The architect wanted to free the philosophy class, its professors and its students, from the inward, cloistered scholasticism that separated esoteric and narrowly focused study from the more quotidian, 'lived world'. It is interesting to compare this with Sen's description of an American visitor's reaction to Tagore's school at Santiniketan. Sen tells us that 'When Tagore established his school he was determined to make it radically different.' He goes on to quote Harvard-educated Joe Marshall's comment, made in 1914, two decades before Sen's birth,

> The principle of [Tagore's] method of teaching is that the individual must be absolutely free and happy in an environment where all is at peace and where the forces of nature are all in evidence; then there must be art, music, poetry, and learning in all its branches in the persons of the teachers; lessons are regular but not compulsory, the classes are held under the trees with the boys sitting at the feet of the teacher, and each student with his different talents and temperament is naturally drawn to the subjects for which he has aptitude and ability.
>
> (Sen 2021, 42)

(This last quote comes from Sen's memoir. The reference given is to Marshall's unpublished, *Santiniketan Journal*.)

Sen goes on to comment on his schooldays at Santiniketan:

> Joe Marshall also commented on Tagore's focus on freedom, even for schoolchildren. This identifies an aspect of Rabindranath's thought that standard accounts, especially those presented by his 'sponsors' in the Western world such as W. B. Yeats and Ezra Pound, missed comprehensively (...) But (...) the idea that the exercise of freedom has to be developed alongside the capacity to reason became increasingly clear to me as my education in Santiniketan proceeded. If you have freedom, you will have reason to exercise it (...) It is the training to make use of the freedom to reason (rather than fearing it, as rote learners are taught to do) that seemed, as my school years proceeded, to be one of the things Tagore was most strongly trying to advance through his unusual school. The exceptional importance of that combination – freedom and reason – has remained with me all my life.
>
> (Sen 2021, 42–3)

Kant and Sen converge upon reason and freedom. Kant thinks that freedom consists in the adherence to rational thought. We are free, only insofar as we are able to release ourselves from the grip of appetite. Sen argues, more relaxedly, that if we are free, we are thereby granted reason to use that freedom. Tagore and Aguirre (the latter as witnessed by Muñoz Molina) converge on the liberation of education from the strictures of the scholastic cloister; both mention their rejection of 'rote learning'; and both see the design of educational settings as a method of establishing that rejection. Previously, we noted Jung's search for the basis of his feeling of *déjà vu*. Sen and Jung agree on other matters concerning the peace we seek between rational participants across national borders. Returning to Delhi to teach economics, philosophy and mathematical logic, from time spent teaching at MIT and Stanford, Sen writes in his preface,

> I decided that there were two quite different ways of thinking about the civilizations of the world. One approach takes the 'fragmentary' perspective and sees a variety of features as manifestations of quite distinct civilizations. This approach, with the additional features of hostility between the fragments, has come much into vogue recently, threatening a lasting 'clash of civilizations'.
>
> The other approach is 'inclusive', and concentrates on looking for different manifestations of ultimately one civilization – which generates different flowers through an interrelated life of roots and branches. This book is not, of course, an investigation of the nature of civilization, but, as the reader will see, its sympathies are with an inclusive rather than a fragmentary understanding of what the world offers.
>
> (Sen 2021, xiv–xv)

Here, assessing the first approach, Sen expresses his anxiety at the rise in populism around the world. Whilst it is a growing problem in the West, it is also manifest in developing nations; and surely Sen must have his worries about the state of Indian politics as now prosecuted. Diminishing resources and increasing poverty worldwide can be seen to fuel protectionism and thereby to push us in the direction of the sort of nationalism that thrives under what Sen describes as the 'fragmentary perspective'.

However, more broadly, we can see in Sen's account of two different ways of thinking, a direct parallel with Auden's two temperaments: the one Arcadian, the other Utopian. In the description of arcadianism, the temperament is that of one who wants return to a land of yore. There is a sort of tribalism in Auden's description of the Arcadian. It is a retrospective position that sees our present condition as having fallen from a glory that is bound up with thoughts of village and nation and defensive rebuttal of all things which threaten from beyond. It seeks to shore up family, village and nation as they are employed to provide an image of self. It is inward looking, rather than expansive. Such a temperament seeks not reasons, which operate on us from without, but rather finds comfort in the familiar. The individual finds home in tradition as that is bequeathed by her forebears. The British distrust of intellectualism is fuelled by its distrust of change inherent in the Utopian temperament. What Sen recognizes in Tagore's (and which we can also recognize in Aguirre's) innovative educational strategies is a reasoned argument for the freedom of education provided in the Bangladeshi children's school, on the one hand; and in the philosopher's seminar room in Madrid, on the other. The distrust of change with its subsequent attachment to convention is a naturalistic view. It is as natural as hefting to a landscape. It is not to be explained by reason-giving, but rather by appeal to our natures. (*This is how* we *have always done it.*) That is to say, it is adopted for no *reason*, and without question. The inclusive, reason-giving view, by contrast, *asks* if education would not be better served by changing, developing or reforming, what had previously been mechanistically practised.

Jung, in his African travels, recalls (if in somewhat extravagant terms) his visit to New Mexico and his conversation with the pueblo Indian, Ochwiay Biano:

> The cosmic meaning of consciousness became overwhelmingly clear to me. 'What nature leaves imperfect, art perfects,' say the alchemists. Man, I, in an invisible act of creation put the stamp of perfection on the world by giving it objective existence. This act we usually ascribe to the Creator alone, without considering that in so doing we view life as a machine calculated down to the last detail, which, along with the human psyche, runs on senselessly, obeying foreknown and predetermined rules. In such a cheerless clockwork fantasy there is no drama of man, world and God; there is no 'new day' leading to 'new shores', but only the dreariness of calculated processes. My old Pueblo friend came to mind. He thought that the *raison d'être* of his pueblo had been to help their father, the sun, to cross the sky each day. I had envied him for the fullness of meaning in that belief, and had been looking about without hope for a myth of our own. Now I knew what it was, and knew even more: that man is

> indispensable for the completion of creation; that, in fact, he himself is the second creator of the world, who alone has given to the world its objective existence – without which, unheard, unseen, silently eating, giving birth, dying, heads nodding through millions of years, it would have gone on in the profoundest night of non-being down to its unknown end. Human consciousness created objective existence and meaning, and man found his indispensable place in the great process of being.
>
> (Jung 2019, 303–4)

The division between Sen's two 'approaches', the fragmentary and the inclusive; and its counterpart in the division between Auden's two 'temperaments', the Arcadian and the Utopian offer up a choice: primitivism and fear or reason and hope.

Kant reconciles the difference between the two perspectives identified by Sen. Again, we shall look into the reconciliation when we look at Kant's conception of cognition in Chapter 4. However, for now, we can say that the more abstract thought becomes, the easier it is to subsume the fragments of the first perspective under the overarching predispositions of the latter. As an example, we might notice that combatants in religious wars each think they have God on their side. However, the two views are incoherent. An all-powerful, all-seeing, all-loving God – the God whom peoples of the book worship – would only want peace. He could not feasibly come down on the side of Jew, Christian or Muslim. Thus, something other than divisions within theological dogma must motivate the combatants in their striving for victory at the others' expense. Establishing commonalities within the doctrines of the book will only help the perspectives converge and should enable the antagonists to better understand each other. At least it would enable them to locate their adversarial points of contention, the better to seek compromise. Therein lies the possibility of reasoned resolution.

Even if such a revelatory argument – that God cannot be rationally held to support either belligerent in a religious conflict, at least the uncovering of the inconsistency demands acknowledgement of some alternative motive – such as greed, power or both.

Sen, writing in 2021, goes on,

> From the crusades in the Middle Ages to the Nazi invasions in the last century, from communal clashes to battles between religious

> politics, there have been tussles between varying convictions, and yet there have also been forces for unity working against those clashes. We can see, if we look, how understanding can spread from one group to another and from one country to the next. As we move around, we cannot escape clues to broader and more integrative stories. Our ability to learn from each other must not be underestimated.
>
> (Sen 2021, xv)

It was before the Nazi atrocities in the thirties and early forties that Jung visited New Mexico and, whilst there, had that conversation with Ochwiay Biano. Jung, in his autobiography, is trying to reconcile two conflicting *feelings*. The one is his sense of belonging to the West, a post-industrial modernist of the enlightenment, whilst at the same time recognizing the power of myth as a means of binding a pre-enlightenment community into a coherent life that fits that community into the world. That sense of *déjà vu* he felt on seeing the Maasai hunter in Kenya unnerves him. The visit to New Mexico was in the same year. Here, in 1925, he meets Ochwiay Biano, who speaks to Jung,

> The whites always want something; they are always uneasy and restless. We do not know what they want. We do not understand them. We think they are mad.
>
> I asked him why he thought the whites were all mad.
>
> 'They think with their heads,' he replied.
>
> 'Why of course. What do you think with?' I asked him in surprise.
>
> 'We think here,' he said, indicating his heart.
>
> I fell into a long meditation. For the first time in my life, so it seemed to me, someone had drawn for me a picture of the real white man. It was as though until now I had seen nothing but sentimental, prettified colour prints. This Indian had struck our vulnerable spot, unveiled a truth to which we are blind. I felt rising within me like a shapeless mist something unknown and yet deeply familiar. And out of this mist, image upon image detached itself: first Roman legions smashing into the cities of Gaul, and the keenly incised features of Julius Caesar, Scipio Africanus, and Pompey. I saw the Roman eagle on the North Sea and on the banks of the White Nile. Then I saw St Augustine

> transmitting the Christian creed to the Britons on the tips of the Roman lances, and Charlemagne's most forced conversions of the heathen; then the pillaging and murdering hands of the Crusading armies. With a stab I realised the hollowness of that old romanticism about the Crusades.
>
> (Jung 2019, 295–6)

In the last chapter we counterposed life in the theatre of war with life embraced in harmony. Peace and culture thrive in unison. Jung's 'colour prints' suggest the sentimentality of a narrative screen overlaid upon the war crimes (if they be so) that Jung goes on to enumerate. Along with Sen, he thinks ill of the crusades and regards the 'old romanticism' as a superstructural dissemblance, a collusion designed to conceal the less glorious ambitions that sat deep beneath the 'colour prints' of a holy war – with God on each side. The enlightenment, for Jung amongst modernists more broadly, serves to evaporate that dissemblance, clearing our vision and bringing into focus the real ambitions that fetched these wars upon us. (This is not to argue there aren't just wars. It is just to argue that many, if not most, are prosecuted for reasons – unethical reasons – that are obscured because, if otherwise clarified, they would be unacceptable.) In Chapter 1, we looked at Paris and Stalingrad during times of war. We looked at how conflict reduced life to mere existence, to the hardship of subsistence. We did this in order to see how its opposite condition is that in which mere existence can be lifted to a level in which we rejoice.

II Socrates, Tagore, Aguirre and Archigram

Jung is cause for curiosity. We have seen that he believes himself to be a follower of Kant. And in *Jung and the Post-Jungians* (Samuels 1986) we are told that Jung's archetypes are descended from Kant's categories. This seems to me to be interestingly wrong. If the archtypes are as the categories, then they figure as *a priori* concepts. However, Jung's archtypes are recruited to a quite different task. Whereas Kant uses the *a priori* concepts, for instance, 'substance' and 'cause' as those concepts under which all experience must be subsumed, Jung uses the archetypes as pre-dispositional accommodations directed towards experiences for which we are in search of explanation. For Kant, if I recognize something and conceive it as a pen (to take an innocuous example), then I see it under the broader concept of an artefact; that in turn under the concept of a thing; and then under the concept of a substance. At this point there is no more general, no wider, more abstract concept than that of a substance. Moreover, if I am writing with that pen, then what I am doing falls under the concept of an action, and that under the concept of an event, which in turn falls under the concept of a cause; beyond which I cannot abstract. So Kant thought that 'substance' and 'cause' were two amongst other *a priori* concepts that together comprise the twelve categories. These two categories are fundamental to Kant's system of cognition, for they pre-exist all of the concepts we derive from experience. (Hence, their *a priori* status.) Their significance is that each inheres in every conception of the world that we might develop through experience. (In the very concept of a pen, the idea of substance inheres. In the very concept of writing, the concept of cause inheres.)

Samuels introduces the notion of archetypes here,

> [A]rchetypal theory provides a crucial link between nature and nurture, inner and outer, scientific and metaphorical, personal and collective or societal.
>
> (Samuels 1986, 23)

And then, in citing Kant as one of Jung's antecedents, he remarks,

> Kant was [an] influence; if knowledge depends on perception, then a notion of perception must precede the acquisition of knowledge. From this idea of an *a priori* perceptive 'form', Kant produced an *a priori* schema in which all sensory data could be organised in fundamental, innate categories. Kantian categories are not passive conceptions; they enter into the composition and constitution of whatever is presented to the senses. They are therefore part of experiencing and, in that sense, close to Jung's definition of archetypes. But Kantian categories are also located beyond time and space and lack a connection to bodily realities and everyday experience.
>
> (Samuels 1986, 23)

Doubts can be raised concerning Samuels' understanding of Kant's categories and his conception of Kant's theory of cognition. Indeed, we shall raise them in due course. However, his conception of Jung's theory of archetypes can be put under scrutiny to advantage. Samuels thinks of archetypes as *a priori* modes of thought, hence explaining the collective nature of our conceptual grasp of certain experiences – why we, different people, converge to a large extent in our mythologizing experiences for which we have no ready scientific explanation.

However, unlike Kant's categories, the archetypes, we must think, are not removed from our bodily realities, nor do they lack connection with everyday experience. Indeed, it is for such experiences as lack scientific explanation that we turn to mythology. In his introduction to *The Essential Jung*, Anthony Storr writes of the archetypes,

> Jung described the collective unconscious as consisting of mythological motifs or primordial images to which he gave the name 'archetypes'. Archetypes are not inborn ideas, but 'typical forms of behaviour which, once they become conscious, naturally present themselves *as ideas and images*, like everything else that becomes a content of consciousness.' (…) Archetypes are not themselves conscious, but seem to be like underlying ground themes upon which conscious manifestations are sets of variations. Their presence is felt as 'numinous'; that is, of profound spiritual significance.
>
> (Storr 1998, 16)

This interpretation of the archetypes best suits the view that we are pre-dispositionally given to mythical accounts of those aspects of experience we cannot understand. Whereas the enlightened will look to science to account for the vagaries, perhaps unprecedented, that befall us, the primordial tendency is to look to mythical explanation.

Consider the problem of evil. Supposing a wicked man murders someone out of sheer spite. The modernist will ask rhetorically: How, if there is a God, could He allow this man to perpetrate such a crime against another who is both innocent and good? In asking this question he is supposing the answer will be that God, in his infinite power to make a world as he wishes, would not make such a world, when He could make a better world – a world in which no such evil exists. However, the reply might well be provided that God, in His wisdom, deems it a better world if we are born free. In granting us our freedom, He makes a world in which we can choose right from wrong.

The second question immediately follows from the first. If God permits persons, in their superior state of freedom, to commit their wicked sins, why has He also created a world in which natural evil occurs? Events of this type are natural disasters, including freak weather conditions that cause loss of life; dreadful diseases that cost lives, conditions which entail severe hardship for those whose lives are, simply as a matter of luck, in the wrong place at the wrong time. The traditional answer to this is that we, the wretched of the earth, limited in our grasp of all things, cannot know the mind of God.

These two versions of the problem of evil are biblical, and anyone who is 'a follower of the book' will recognize the profundity of the question in each version and the awesome vision of the power of God that each entails.

The purpose with which I bring these into our discussion is to show what it is to be pre-disposed to give a certain account of the phenomena that we recognize in these examples. We are pre-disposed to think that there must be a *reason* for the terrible phenomena we encounter. The enlightened thinker will simply search out a scientific explanation of why some natural disaster has befallen some individual or some community. That is to search out a *natural cause*. In searching out a *reason*, the pre-modern is asking *who* did this? Who is responsible for this? In so doing, the search is for some form of agency – an agency more powerful than human being. ('Why did God permit the wicked man to murder his victim?' asks for an explanation that imputes agency to a most powerful being. It is a question in search of a myth.)

So archetypical are such searches for human meaning that the instances across cultures converge upon a single archetype. Thus monotheistic cultures rely upon a supreme being, whilst polytheistic cultures have multiple agencies, each greater than ours but none supremely powerful, and hence these gods have their own lives to lead. On this polytheistic view the gods are persons too; they have reasons for acting both with respect to their fellow gods and with respect to us.

What this view of the archetypes supports is the idea that there are anthropological convergences which are to be accounted for by our condition as pre-disposed persons. It funds the view that there are commonalities between communities. Let us consider, again, the convergence of the view that education might be better exercised in a setting that is continuous with nature, or with the continuity of the classroom with life pursued around it. Aguirre's design permits the students and their professors to look out upon the landscape so as not to seclude their reflections within the confines of the classroom. Sen delights in the boys sitting at the feet of their teachers outdoors at Santiniketan. In Plato's *Phædrus*, Socrates is prowling about the streets of Athens when he meets Phædrus, the boy excited having just come from a speech by the rhetorician Lysias. Phædrus has a copy of the speech under his cloak and so Socratres asks him to walk outside the walled city so they can find a suitable resting place, where Phædrus can read the speech to Socrates. Phædrus finds a spot:

> Socrates: well really, this is a glorious resting-place. For the plane-tree I find is thick and spreading, as well as tall, and the size and the shadiness of the agnus castus here is very beautiful, and being at the height of its flower, it must render our retreat most fragrant. How delicious too is this spring trickling under the plane-tree, and how cold is the water, to judge by the foot! It would seem from these images and votive offerings that the place is sacred to some nymphs and river-god. Again, how lovely and enjoyable above measure is the airiness of the spot! summer-like and clear there rings an answer to the choir of cicalas. But the most charming thing of all is this abundant grass, with its gentle slope just made for the head to fall back on luxuriously. Really, Phædrus, you make a most admirable guide.
>
> (Plato 1927, 230)

Phædrus proceeds to read the speech by Lysias whilst, in the setting described, Socrates lies on the grass listening to his young friend.

What is striking about this passage is its architectural quality. The description of the temperature, the comfortable grass, the sounds of the running spring and the chorus of the cicadas, all add to the experience we imagine Socrates undergoing as those environmental qualities add to, rather than detract from, Socrates pleasure in thinking about the speech rehearsed by Phædrus.

That dialogue was composed by Plato around 370 BCE. Compare that to an advertisement for an early portable Sony television set; the black-and-white photograph conscripted by Archigram as an example how architecture might be conceivably pursued. Archigram believed, like many optimists, that technology would lend our lives ease; and that this, in turn, would make our lives better to both create and appreciate an appropriately modernized culture. Such a modern world, as envisaged by Archigram, could be sustained without walls, and without the formality and 'rationalism' of modern architecture. It would look like the backdrop of the dialogue in which Socrates and Phædrus enjoyed an afternoon thinking about the abstract nature of love and beauty. (Though, of course, our Greek philosophers were undistracted by the conveniences of modern technology.) And so the photographic television advertisement unwittingly gave us an image of how such a life might be enjoyed. Wittingly, Greene appropriated the photograph, cutting it from its advertising context and pasting it into Archigram's manifesto, where it was to sit surrounded by the text of Greene's, *Bottery*, a piece of prose poetry in which the photograph appears. The text includes, 'DEFINITIONS: a Bottery is a fully serviced landscape' (Greene 1999, 144).

Notwithstanding the technological discrepancy between our two cases, there are ways in which we can appreciate the setting of the dialogue from an architectural point of view. And Greene's *Bottery* is a persuasion to this end. In the passage quoted above, in praise of the beauty of the place that Phædrus has chosen for the discourse, Socrates mentions several times the functional qualities that the place has in terms of the comfort it affords. So, the projection of architectural qualities is exhibited in the appraisal of the site discussed by the two interlocutors, an appraisal of its fittingness for the afternoon's unfolding. It is also with *The Phædrus*, we can frame the teaching ambience at Sen's school in Santiniketan.

Mention of the projection of architectural qualities alerts us to the relationship between our experience of beauty and the environment from which that experience derives. Looking for a suitable habitat outside the walls of Athens is a search for what fits.

PART TWO

The system of the (fine) arts

3

The fine art members' club: Architecture's candidature

I The modern system of the arts

As far back as Aristotle, philosophers had thought mimesis was the way to characterize a number of disparate competences, some of which, we now regard as arts. Plato had dismissed poetry and painting as dissembling pursuits, removing ideas yet further from reality. Platonic ideas are pure forms. These pure forms are the ultimate constituents of reality. Objects as they appear to us in the world, beds for instance, are an agglomeration of individuals, each of which is mimetic of the pure form. They thereby partake in that form in some way. The pure form is the idea: *bedness*. So, *bedness* the pure form, inheres in each and every bed. A representation of a bed, say a painting, is a mimetic copy of the individual bed, itself mimetic of the pure form. Thus, the mimetic painting moves us still further from reality than when we were looking at individual beds – those objects that furnish our homes and in which we sleep, read the papers, shout at the dog, indulge in champagne and scrambled egg breakfasts on our birthdays; listen to the wireless news of a morning; watch a late-night movie on the television; squander hours in them with our paramours; etc. We are born in beds. We convalesce in them. We die in them. We can do none of these things in a painting of a bed. (On the other hand, one can only wonder what Plato might get up to in his ideal bed.)

Mimesis, for the ancients, was a matter of our grasping the world and centrally included the notion of sense perception. Goran Sörböm, in his 'The Classical Concept of Mimesis', writes,

> In the classical period (...) (t)he basic metaphor used to characterize this process [visual perception] was that of pressure. [When we see a house] [a]n individual thing presses its contingent qualities and shapes upon the senses like a signet ring which, when stamped into wax, delivers its form but not its matter to the wax. However, when we think 'house' the mind entertains the essence, real nature of the 'houseness of houses' which is something general and not accessible to the senses (*aesthesis*) but only to thought (*noesis*) since thoughts do not have individual and contingent properties.
>
> (Sörböm 2002, 20)

Perceptions were included in the ancients' inventory of mental images – those passively received and through which we project our intellectual order. It would be eccentric, to say the least, for a contemporary philosopher to count perceptions as mental images since perceptions, unlike mental images, are achievements; perceptions reach out and take hold of reality; whereas, arguably, mental images do not. Perception delivers the world to us. Mental images, as a rule, do not. As Wittgenstein reminds us, we cannot learn from our mental images. They are, in this respect, subject to our will. The content they deliver is the content we invest in them. Such a distinction draws a hard line between perception and imagination, notwithstanding the role Kant has for imagination in the manifold of perception. We shall need to call upon this distinction when we come to assess the role of imagination in our appreciation of architecture.

Aristotle, a student of Plato, by contrast, thought mimesis enabled us to learn about reality. A line drawing, for instance, better reveals the contours of an object than when we encounter the object face-to-face. So, images can tell us something about those things of which they are images. Such a view is not, in itself, *aesthetic*. For it tells us only that line drawings, for instance, can have a role to play in our grasp of reality. They are, thus employed, epistemic tools.

The ancients did not have a conception of fine art comparable to that of the modern era. We translate the Greek '*techne*' as 'art', but it is more accurately translated as 'skill' or 'technique'. So, whilst mimesis groups together ways in which the world might be copied, it does not follow that this was a criterion of what it was for a thing to be a work of art in our sense, nor yet that it was a way of creating and appreciating beauty. 'Aesthetics' derives from the Greek words, *aisthanesthai*, to perceive; and *aisthētica*, things perceptible. It was not until the eighteenth century that Alexander Gotlieb Baumgarten gave the name to the philosophical study of beauty. Nevertheless, the influence of the ancients, and of Aristotle in particular, pressed upon those who later wanted to develop a unified theory of the arts.

'Is architecture a fine art?' This remains our central question. Since antiquity, separate skills had each been given their own characterization and were, therefore, a disorganized agglomeration of disjunctive pursuits. In the eighteenth century, however, succeeding Diderot's *Encyclopaedia*, effort had been put into unifying these accounts according to some underlying system; a structure designed to discriminate which objects could be ruled into, and which should be ruled out of, its various classifications of *art*.

According to Abbé Charles Batteaux, the 'Fine Arts' were grouped together principally as those affording pleasure. The fine arts in their plurality, on such a view, are unified in *our* psychological apprehension of, and attitude directed upon, each. That is, it is *the mode of attention* we pay towards the arts that provides the unity. Hence, it is supposed to have provided a systematic and unifying explanation of the fine arts. It is also supposed to have distinguished between these and the other arts, for instance the mechanical arts, differentiated by their utility. To this he adds a third category, the 'beautifying arts' which have both pleasure and utility as their determining character.

Batteux, nevertheless, sought to account for the fine arts by adopting the classical notion of mimesis. Thus, he sought the unity of the arts out there, in a single property, or group thereof, by which they are assembled. With mimesis – now the purported criterion for a thing's being a work of fine art – drama, poetry, painting and sculpture were well accommodated. They are simply beautiful objects in virtue of imitating, in some specified way, beautiful nature. Music and architecture are left wondering how they might fit in. According to Aristotle, music is imitative of human character. In book XIX, 'Problems Connected with Music', Aristotle asks,

> Why is it that of all things which are perceived by the senses that which is heard alone possesses character? For music, even if it is unaccompanied by words, yet has character; whereas a colour and an odour and a savour have not. Is it because that which is

> heard alone has movement (...)? This does not occur in the other objects of sense perception. Now these movements are connected with action, and actions are indicative of character.
>
> (Aristotle 1984b, 1434)

Sörbom, in his essay, quotes Aristotle, who wrote 'musical times and tunes provide us with images [*homoiomata, likenesses*] of states of character' (Sörbom 2002, 23).
Sörbom continues,

> When we say 'the piece of music is sad', this means in terms of the theory of *mimesis* that the piece of music generates a mental image of sadness in the listener's mind in a similar way as a painting can represent, i.e. generate a mental image of, a house without being a house.
>
> (Sörbom 2002, 23)

Thus, Batteux is enabled to account for our notion of musical expression, for it can now be subsumed under mimesis and, therefore, music finds a pathway into his newly unified theory of the fine arts. The significance of this for architecture is, therefore, welcome. Music is an abstract art, and so its admission into the mimetic arts opens the way for architecture. How so? We must return to this question in the next section. For now we will turn to Paul Oskar Kristeller's 'The Modern System of the Arts'.

As Kristeller puts it, in the *second* part of his review of eighteenth-century thinkers,

> The decisive step toward a system of the fine arts was taken by the Abbe Batteux in his famous and influential treatise, '*Les beaux-arts réduit à un mème principe*' (1746). It is true that many elements of his system were derived from previous authors, but at the same time it should not be overlooked that he was the first to set forth a clearcut system of the fine arts in a treatise devoted exclusively to this subject.
>
> (Kristeller 1952, 20)

According to Batteux, the fine arts were held to include music, poetry, painting, sculpture and the dance. Unfortunately, the exclusion of architecture from this list makes moot the answer to our question concerning its status as a fine art. However, better news precedes Kristeller's survey of thinkers in part II of his essay. A year earlier, in the *first*, of his two-part essay, he had written,

> Although the terms 'Art,' 'Fine Arts' or 'Beaux Arts' are often identified with the visual arts alone, they are also quite commonly understood in a broader sense. In this broader meaning, the term 'Art' comprises above all the five major arts of painting, sculpture, architecture, music and poetry. These five constitute the irreducible nucleus of the modern system of the arts, on which all writers and thinkers seem to agree.
>
> (Kristeller 1951, 497)

Splendid. We have an answer to the question posed as to whether architecture is a fine art. *It is*. However, Kristeller's detractors can point to the fact that architecture, since Vitruvius, has been considered in terms of its practical function. Vitruvius, we should remember, had demanded that architecture contain '*firmitas, utilitas, et venustas*' (structural strength, function and beauty). That seems reasonable enough, but how does each contained feature relate to, or depend upon, another? A residual problem is Batteux's inclusion of the third characterization of the arts in general as, 'the beautifying arts'. These, by definition, lie beyond his system of the 'fine arts', precisely because they have utility as a component feature. Batteux, as we noted, was a classicist and, as such, would have wanted to adapt his system to incorporate and explain the centrality of mimesis. Accordingly he would have recourse to Aristotle, who writes at the outset of *The Metaphysics*,

> At first he who invented any art that went beyond the common perceptions of man was naturally admired by men, not only because there was something useful in the inventions, but because he was thought wise and superior to the rest. But as more arts were invented, and some were directed to the necessities of life, others to its recreation, the inventors of the latter were always regarded as wiser than the inventors of the former, because their branches of knowledge did not aim at utility.
>
> (Aristotle 1984a, 981b)

It looks, on the face of it, that such a view throws a spanner in the works for our central ambition: the establishment of architecture as a fine art. Certainly, when we come to discuss function, and thereby utility, we shall have to tackle this problem head on.

Nevertheless, mimesis as a feature of music does not rely upon utility as its motivation. Military music and religious music may recruit the movement of music to their ends, but music is not essentially functional. Aristotle identified movement as locating the shared properties of *mimema* and character. If architecture is to be a fine art under these terms, we shall have to identify the properties shared by the real thing and the mimetic in architecture.

What is the classicist's claim with regard to mimesis? How could architecture be a mimetic art, and thereby secure its place in the fine arts?

II Classicism and mimesis: The primordial hut

A work of architecture, according to many classicists, imitates or represents the primitive form of building; it can also, in so doing, imitate or represent other classical buildings which ultimately derive their form from that of the primitive. The classical 'vocabulary' is thus seen to symbolize the necessities involved in the history of constructing our accommodation. Whether imitating the primitive or the classical, architecture takes as its content the myths involved in and around building.

In William Chambers' *A Treatise on Civil Architecture*, the chapter 'Of the Origin of Buildings' assigns to classical architecture its imitative derivation from the primordial hut. In this he follows eighteenth-century Jesuit priest and architectural historian, Marc-Antoine Laugier. He then goes on to account for the Doric order by illustrating its columns and shows the development of the Corinthian order by illustrating its capital,

This view of the origins and meaning of classicism dates back to Vitruvius. It persists and is alive today in a yet more ambitious form. Here is contemporary classical architect, Demitri Porphyrios,

FIGURE 3.1 *William Chambers, page from* Treatise on Civil Architecture, *1825, Public Domain via Wikimedia Commons.*

> [A] Classicist would argue, architecture is the imitative celebration of construction and shelter qualified by myths and ideas of a given culture. Such myths might have to do with life, nature or the mode of production of a given society. Ultimately, architecture speaks of these myths and ideas but always through the language of construction and shelter by means of tectonic order.
>
> (Porphyrios 1996, 95)

FIGURE 3.2 *Demitri Porphyrios, Battery Park City Pavilion, 2014. © Beyond My Ken, 2014.*

In this construal of the imitation of primitive construction of shelter, Porphyrios broadens the object imitated to include our myths and ideas, but always focused on the tectonic order of that construction. In so doing, the shelter celebrated here is now enabled to form our mythical conception of 'dwelling'; and so the classicist can be credited, if successful, with demonstrating the relationship between dwelling and building. 'Building belongs to dwelling', he will tell us, 'in that it imitates our earliest success in surviving the circumstances into which we have been cast'.

It seems odd, though, to think that mimesis should be so constrained in the case of architecture: that buildings can only imitate buildings. After all, paintings are capable of representing any object in the visual world, and the scenes and events that those objects together comprise. The oddness might be explained by a consideration of the concept in antiquity. Certainly, the ancients distinguished between *mimemata* (the copies) and real things (the copied). They believed that *mimemata* shared with real things, some, but not all, properties. If the *mimema* was to share all its properties with the real thing of which it was intended to be a copy, it would *not* be a copy, but another instance of the real thing. So the building, as *mimema*, would have to have properties the building it copies has not. However, these properties are still properties of a building, since the *mimema* is itself a building. It begins to look as if there are no properties that the *mimema* can have, as *mimema*, that are essentially different from the real thing.

By analogy, we think of the form of a painting, sculpture or poem as distinct from its content. Paintings are patches of pigment suspended in glue across a flat support; sculptures are carved hard inanimate material (stone or wood, for instance) or modelled soft inanimate material (clay or wax, for instance) that represent visual worlds including animate content; poetry is composed in structures which organize content according to independent schemes of meter, assonance, rhyme, tone and colour, amongst other poetic devices. In each case we can give some sort of answer to what independent properties belong to the art in question, but no such analogous set of properties appear to be available to the architect.

To clarify this point, let's make an analogy. This is a recipe for blancmange from the Middle Ages:

> [H]ere you find the version from *Diuersa servicia*, because that is the oldest (1381):
>
> *For to make blomanger of fysch, tak a pound of rys. Les hem wel & wasch, & seþ tyl þey breste & lat hem kele; & do þereto mylk of to pound of almandys. Nym þe perche or þe lopuster & boyle yt, & kest sugur & salt also þerto, & serue yt forth.*
>
> To make blancmange of fish, take a pound of rice. Clean and wash it well, boil until they (the grains) break, and let cool. Add milk of two pounds of almonds. Take perch or lobster and boil it, and cast sugar and salt in also. Serve it forth.
>
> (Coquinaria 2019)

Fish blancmange was served on fast days and during lent. Religious restriction upon eating meat meant that more than half the days of the year were meat-free. Otherwise, the dish would be made with chicken or any white meat.

The oddity now occurs in the following thought experiment. There are many internationally famous milk or cream puddings – *panna cotta*, *crème brûlée*, *crème caramel*, as well as our own blancmange. We might think of them as regional varieties of a custard desert. In tracing the history of blancmange, we might think that our pink strawberry pudding hails from the Middle Ages – from the savoury dish whose recipe is quoted above. But our creamy gelatinous sweet is neither fish nor fowl. No one, so far as I know, has suggested that strawberry blancmange, in order to be appreciated, has to be regarded as imitative of its fourteenth-century precedent. The proof of the blancmange is in the eating. But *should* we also regard it as mimetic of the centuries old plate? If it is a mistake so to think, might we not judge it as an analogous mistake to regard the appreciation of the classical building as dependent upon our recognition of its imitative relation to the primordial hut? The proof of the classical building, it might be suggested, is in its inhabitation; and it is unclear that its inhabitation requires our sustained appreciation of its imitative presentation of the primordial building – either hut or temple.

In comparing *mimemata* to the real things of which they provide us with mental images, we might think it is not that the *mimemata* do not share all the properties of the real things to which they are related. (Although, of course, this is true.) Rather, it is that as *mimemata*, they have essential properties that the real thing does not have, and cannot have. However, the classical building *is a building*. So, no property of the building, as a *mimema*, can be identified that is an essential feature of it as a *mimema* that is independent of its purported reference to the real thing of which it is a *mimema*.

With regard to such reference, it seems absurd to say of someone who fails to see the primitive hut in any classical building that she has failed to understand the building, especially if she feels perfectly at home in its embrace. It is as absurd as saying of someone that, if she fails to connect the reference of the strawberry blancmange to the fish dish from which it derives, she doesn't appreciate it. Appreciation is a mode of understanding. It goes further than merely liking, including, as it does, an estimation of the experience into which she has entered.

Even so, an objection to this argument might still be raised. Isn't the mimic a *real* person impersonating another *real* person? If so, then we could, by further analogy, think of a classical building as an example of mimesis within the art of architecture. This analogy, however, only strengthens the case against mimesis. For the mimic to impersonate another is to draw attention to the difference between mimic (the *mimema*) and the impersonated character.

III The three Rs: Recognition, resistance and representation

Mimesis, whilst appearing to offer hope of a unified system of the arts, fails as an account of what we moderns call representation. For mimesis is a theory of copying, by which attributes of the copied are instantiated in the copy. Robert Ousterhout (1984) describes how, during the Middle Ages, throughout western Europe, there proliferated copies of objects which were thought to be sacred, and the copy was thought to thereby instantiate the holiness of the object copied. The copies, by virtue of instantiating *some* of the properties of the original, contained a degree of the sanctity of the original object. The most frequently copied of buildings during the Middle Ages was the church of the Holy Sepulchre in Jerusalem, which, we have been told, marks the sites of Christ's crucifixion, burial and resurrection. Copies of the church often betray a lack of visual likeness to the original, but the fact that certain features of the original were instantiated in the copy invested the copy with religious significance. The meaning was thought to transcend the visual and to reside in certain numerical and proportional correspondences. These correspondences worked in conjunction with relics and other objects of significance to provide a sacred meaning. The faithful buried in close proximity to a copy of the Holy Sepulchre were offered salvation through the death and resurrection of Christ, made immanent in the architectural copy.

The classicists' attempt to retain mimesis as the central explanatory concept, bringing unity to the arts, can be seen to fail, in retrospect, on two counts. Firstly, as noted above, they search for the unity of the arts in properties of the objects which are its works, rather than in the mental activity appropriate to apprehending beauty. Secondly, in the particular case of representation, they fail because our notion of representation is more finely tuned than was the notion of a copy. (Nevertheless, Porphyrios' account, broadened to include, 'the myths and ideas of a given culture', redeems classicism as a way of making works of architecture. It does not, however, secure the claim that it is the *only* way of making architecture as a fine art.)

Sartre uses the example of the mimic in his exploration of the intentionality of imagination in his *L'Imaginaire* (Sartre 2004). Intentionality is best summarized as the 'directedness of thought', or, in a more Sartrean idiom, 'the directedness of consciousness'. When we direct our consciousness at signs, according to Sartre, we enter into sign consciousness. Signs are indifferent to their objects, being related only by convention. (It is only by convention that 'pan' refers to a cooking vessel in English and to a dietary staple in Spanish.) For Sartre, we grasp the meaning of signs by habit; that is how their objects come before the mind. When we *aim* our consciousness at pictures, we enter into what Sartre calls 'image consciousness'. When I see a photograph of Pierre, and enter into image consciousness, I direct my consciousness towards Pierre – through the picture, as it were. In image consciousness we come to the picture prepared to *see* Pierre. By contrast, when we see the black-and-white photographic print as a monochrome arrangement of tones across a flat surface (ignoring its pictorial content) we enter into 'perception consciousness'. So, in this example, the two intentional contents are distinguished by the different aims we have when entering into either one of these two forms of consciousness. These two modes of directing consciousness determine the appearance of the objects at which we look.

Sartre considers the difference between a painted portrait and the impersonator, Mdme Franconay, who performs her impressions of Maurice Chevalier as part of her stage act:

> The difference between the consciousness of imitation and the consciousness of a portrait comes from the difference in matter. The matter of the portrait itself solicits the spectator to effect the synthesis, because the painter has given a perfect resemblance to the subject. The matter of the imitation is a human body. It is rigid, it resists.
>
> (Sartre 2004, 26)

By this resistance, we can take Sartre to mean that the mimic stubbornly refuses to disappear. She insists upon her presence.

The persistent presence of the mimic in the foreground thereby precludes access to unobtruded image consciousness. The resistance, as it were, forbids the synthetic convergence of the two modes of consciousness; so that we cannot pass from the one, perception, to the other, image. Sartre continues,

> The imitator is small, stout, brunette; a woman, she imitates a man. The result is that the imitation is *approximate*. The object that Franconay produces by means of her body is a feeble form, which can always be interpreted in two distinct ways: I am always free to see Maurice Chevalier as imaged, or a small woman pulling faces [as perceived]. From this it follows the essential role of signs: they must enlighten and guide consciousness.
>
> (Sartre 2004, 26)

In contrast to the mimic's imitation, Sartre writes that 'the painter has given a perfect resemblance'. This can only make sense if we regard the seeing of the content in the picture as a different sort of seeing (consciousness) than that of perceiving the flat picture. Just two pages earlier in his account of portrayal he has written,

> I think, let us say, of Pierre in the picture. This means that I do not think of the picture at all: I think of Pierre. One should not therefore believe that I think of the picture 'as an image of Pierre'. This is a reflective consciousness that reveals the function of the picture in my present consciousness. For the reflective consciousness, Pierre and the picture are two distinct objects. But in the imaging attitude, the picture is nothing but a way for Pierre to appear to me as absent. So the picture *gives* Pierre, though Pierre is not there.
>
> (Sartre 2004, 24)

Sartre uses different modes of consciousness as we might think of distinguishing the uses of images in our human commerce. It is true that we look at pictures and regard other representations according to the projects to which they are conscripted. There is a difference in the phenomenology of looking at a picture according to whether we want to locate a missing person; to choose a summer cardigan; to capture something of the horror of a natural disaster; to solve the puzzle (hopefully) of how to put a flat-pack piece of furniture together, or to reflect upon the aesthetic merit of a landscape painting. The image is to be brought before the mind in different ways. When looking at pornographic imagery, the consumer masks out of his experience the presence of the inked printed page or the pixelated screen (unless he has, peculiarly, fetishized the fragrance of the ink or the flicker of the screen, and is no longer attentive to the pictorial content). More usually, when looking at the football match on the television, for instance, the screen hardly intrudes upon our project. We pass from one perception of a flat rectangle against a wall to the moving image of a football match. Perhaps to render it in terms more likely to capture Sartre's usage, we see no television, our consciousness is fully occupied with the unfolding game.

It is interesting that Sartre is writing about imagination and its role in depiction. However, from an *aesthetic* point of view we need to look particularly at premeditated aesthetic pictures, pictures made intentionally to provide aesthetic value. We need to see why it is that some pictures are works of art, whilst others are not. We need, that is, to separate out a general theory of depiction (if there is one) from an account of how some pictures have a special *aesthetic* significance for us. In pursuing this exercise, we shall stride down a well-trodden path, in the hope of developing analogies for use in our efforts to supply a description of the medium of architecture.

Wollheim, more than any other philosopher, has shaped our thinking about the *aesthetics* of painting. In his espousal of the 'twofold thesis', he lays out the grounds for what it is to have an aesthetic interest in painting (Wollheim 1987). The thesis claims that when appreciating paintings, my attention is distributed between looking at the flat surface and seeing in that surface a representational effect. It is precisely in this distribution of attention to the two folds of our experience that we achieve what Sartre calls a synthesis. However, the complex experience comprising two folds prohibits our looking through the picture to Sartre's 'perfect resemblance'. Perhaps Sarte is right about the other forms of image consciousness, but our concern is with aesthetics. Whilst the distribution of attention to the two folds can, in different instances of painting, vary in predominance, at no point can either fold be attenuated to the point of evaporation. Both folds are essential to the complex aesthetic experience of looking at paintings. (Of course, I could look at a seventeenth-century painting to discover what costume a Dutch captain might wear in a shooting party, and I could look to see which of a variety of paintings had sufficient red to go with the interior of my living room, but these acts of attention to one or the other fold would not count as an *aesthetic* interest in the work, *as a painting*.)

Thus, (*pace* Sartre) in painting, it is a certain 'resistance' that is *required* to take an aesthetic interest. That resistance shows up in our appreciation of the work in painting. It is the point at which we attend to the exploitation of the medium. We move onto this point later in this chapter where we look at Lopes' insistence on medium specificity for each art-kind, as a pre-requisite for a work being a *work* of an art-kind.

Whilst the distinction between impersonation and portraiture is interesting, in that it could be recruited to advance a theory of depiction, our interest in it is focused on the restriction it places upon impersonation as mimesis. For, if Sartre offers a good description of the resistance of the mimic, her refusal to disappear from our attention, of her persistence in consciousness, then we have reason to think that architecture, considered exclusively as an imitative art, would do little to establish its credentials as a fine art. After all, impersonation is not included in the system of fine arts, and mimicry is beginning to look like the most plausible candidate for the kind of mimesis engaged by architecture

Thus, either we need to review our position that architecture is a fine art; or we need to abandon the classicists' categorization of the fine arts – abandon their adherence to the mimetic thesis and reconsider the constitution of the fine arts.

IV Wherein lies the unity of the fine arts?

Wollheim has leaned on the notion that artists work within a conception of the specific kind of art they practise. If that is so, perhaps we should focus upon the individual art-kinds and not on some overarching scheme that provides either systematic unity. Perhaps Batteaux' adherence to the classical conception of mimesis was mistaken in that it demanded that each art should in some way exhibit the same property whatever the prevailing characteristics of the specific art under view. Instead of looking for a single shared property, we might better look to establish a regulatory theory for each of the fine arts. Wollheim:

> A preliminary point is that the fact that paintings and poems belong to the categories they do is not simply an observational fact – though it is also that (…) The truth is that Verdi composed his operas under the concept 'opera': the concept was regulative for what he wrote, and I shall express the point by saying that it formed part of the 'artist's theory' which governed his creativity. This point may be generalized, so that we may think of the artist's theory under which each artist works as containing a concept of the kind of work of art he is engaged in producing, and this concept will necessarily include reference to the category to which this work belongs (…)
>
> (Wollheim 1980, 171)

For each art, I take it, there is to be some characterization of what constitutes its practice, and, by extension, what constitutes its appreciation. And if Wollheim's preliminary point is correct, we should expect each art's characterization to reveal for us the assumptions that should, in the most general way, set limits to the thought experiments we make concerning the arts. Concerned with the art of poetry, T. S. Eliot writes of the constraint upon modernity exerted by tradition (Eliot 1988). Each artist must fit herself into the history of her particular art. In so doing, she adjusts that history, renewing it, refreshing it and readjusting it. Her work is thereby *situated*.

In that same paper, Eliot argues against the importance of recognizing the artist's intention. His argument is orthodox for the time. The view is that perceptual features of the work of art are those to which we respond. The work's history is not a perceptible feature of the work itself – it is external to it – and so cannot be called upon to fund our aesthetic experience.

These two points sit ill at ease with each other. The first, whilst attractive as an account across the arts, has its own problems. The second is, whilst the first is not, almost entirely wrong. Let's take them one at a time. Eliot attempts in this section to contrive a reconciliation between the history of poetry and the work of the contemporary poet as she seeks to find her place in that history.

In painting, by analogy, the spectator's willed experience includes attention to features of the paint surface in her achieving her aesthetic experience. Those features would be excluded from, masked out of, her experience were she to direct it towards another pictorial ambition. It is here we recognize Eliot's claim that artists situate their work within tradition in such a way that spectators can appreciate their contribution. The viewer's imaginative experience of the work places it within or against other works and thereby sees it as striking an attitude to those other works. It is as if each work gestures towards other works and that recognizing these gestures affords one dimension along which meaning in the arts can be developed and appreciated. Wollheim and Eliot together provide ample resources for an account of the importance of assumption and expectation in our appreciation of works of art within a specified medium.

It is worth looking in detail at what Eliot says about poetry:

> No poet, no artist of any art, has his complete meaning alone. His significance, his appreciation is the appreciation of his relation to the dead poets and artists. You cannot value him alone; you must set him, for contrast and comparison, among the dead. I mean this as a principle of æsthetic, not merely historical criticism. The necessity that he shall conform, that he shall cohere, is not one-sided; what happens when a new work of art is created is something that happens simultaneously to all the works of art which preceded it. The existing monuments form an ideal order among themselves, which is modified by the introduction of the new (the really new) work of art among them. The existing order is complete before the new work arrives; for order to persist after the supervention of novelty, the *whole* existing order must be, if ever so slightly, altered; and so the relations, proportions, values of each work of art toward the whole are readjusted; and this is conformity between the old and the new. Whoever has approved this idea of order, of the form of European, of English literature, will not find it preposterous that the past should be altered by the present as the present is directed by the past. And the poet who is aware of this will be aware of great difficulties and responsibilities.
>
> (Eliot 1975, 38)

Whilst Eliot writes of poetry, he also acknowledges that 'no artist of any art, has his meaning alone'. Nevertheless, he is not offering a comprehensive account of art *simpliciter*. Rather, it is up to any artist of any art, that she should immerse herself in the history of *that art*, within which she seeks accommodation.

A difficulty arrives with the view that contemporary art not only has the power to change the art of the past, but that it is required to so do. For, we might pre-philosophically presume that the meaning or significance of a work of art, even its beauty, is a result of what the artist intended to do when making the work. However, if that is so, it is difficult to grant Eliot's claim that the contemporary work can alter the art of the past, since the dead cannot be said to have intended the new manifestation of their work in light of the contemporary world. If Frank Auerbach, for instance, is said to change the way we look at Rembrandt, then it cannot have been Rembrandt's intention that we look at the seventeenth-century painting with our contemporary gaze. For, Rembrandt cannot have foreseen the new light that shines upon his work. It is, after all, *ex hypothesi*, that the novelty of the new is the sole guarantee of its contemporary relevance.

The second point, which Eliot develops from his first, is that the artist has no knowledge of her intention in making a piece of art. However, having no knowledge of an intention does not, in and of itself, rule out the presence of intentions. We need not subscribe to a fully blown psychoanalytic theory to concede this. We often do things, not knowing why we do them, whilst conceding that we did them intentionally. Indeed, if we think of improvisation in the arts, unknown (perhaps unknowable) intentions provide best explanations for what appears. Moreover, these explanations, we hope, are the best available, *rational* explanations for the manifestations we encounter. Take, for one example: free jazz.

This, however, is true in what might, on first blush, appear to be a more deliberate example of art-making. The poet considers her words, looks for rhyme, meter, sound patterns, amongst other things. From whence do they emerge? Even if not always, they appear *impromptu*. Suddenly, she spontaneously solves a specific poetic problem. The painter looks at her painting, smoking a cigarette, drinking a coffee, looking and looking again. Why does it take time for her to suddenly leap towards the canvas and make a change? Why does it not appear to her as if she has been consulting a dictionary to see what a particular word means? It is because there is a simple process of looking up a word. We go to the dictionary and find it alphabetically. Then we read it off. But what happens when the painter decides, of a sudden, that a mark needs exaggeration or a change of tone? (Do not posit a *homunculus* here.) The painter makes mistakes. She corrects them as she goes. The marks she makes won't do.

This is true of all the arts. The procedure of tentatively putting something forward, adjusting it, erasing parts, adding others, replacing pieces of the work, until the artist arrives at what she intended; even if she could not have said, in advance, what it was at which she was aiming. Indeed, we find the free jazz example more perplexing because it stands as it comes, uncorrected. The football match is yet another example. Where players try and co-ordinate moves that sometimes fail to succeed; at other times they do. Ask the sportswoman what she was doing. There need be nothing going through her mind. And yet what she does, she does intentionally.

The process of making architecture is complex and shares with other disciplines the need for others to participate. We saw in Chapter 1, the descriptions of the various aptitudes that the fictional architect Ignacio Abel called upon in his work at University City in Madrid. Muñoz Molina writes of Abel's sense of line and his love of making marks on the paper; of his knowing the feel of stone in the hands of a mason, the carpenter's skill that he, Abel, does not have. Thus, like other arts that require the coordination and cooperation of other skilled artisans, the architect has to manage a workforce put in place to realize her vision.

The fact that the architect is not, physically, the maker of the work, cannot count against her. She needs to be able to draw, to make models, to realize – to manifest – an idea. It is then she needs to manage the fulfilment of the idea in its built form.

V Van Eck on Alberti

The question, as to whether to grant architecture such status was addressed by Alberti in his *On the Art of Building in Ten Books*; and so, we shall dip our toes into history in order to see what he thought; and to see whether it casts light on our discussion. Our guide for this excursion shall be the contemporary art historian, Caroline van Eck (1999).

Eck resists the usual interpretation of Alberti as conceiving architecture in historical, that is classical, terms. Instead she writes,

> Alberti's evident concern for the survival of classical architecture has obscured one very interesting feature of his theory of architecture, *viz.* that his analysis of architecture is conducted entirely in a-historical and a-stylistic terms. Nature, not classical antiquity, is the final authority. This is shown by his definition of architecture, his analysis of the design process, his conceptualisation of the orders and his definition of beauty.
>
> (van Eck 1999, 119)

In an assessment of architecture and its possible manifestations, it would be ill-considered to reject classicism as one – notwithstanding some of the hastier claims of the modernist, if we take them at face value, rather than as polemic in favour of 'the new'. Thus, 'Alberti's evident concern' need not be harnessed to the cause as an argument for architecture's identity as exclusively classical. That said, it would be implausible to retaliate by excluding classicism from such an identity as we seek. Nevertheless, if architecture is to be regarded as a fine art, we might reasonably expect that the architect fight shy of adherence to dogmatic classical constraints; but she might find that within classicism, there are opportunities to exploit creative design. On this matter, we should keep our minds open.

Famously, as we have seen, Vitruvius wrote that architecture should exhibit *firmitas*, *utilitas* and *venustas* (structural strength, utility and beauty), and that aphorism remains at the heart of architectural thinking to this day. However, as it stands, Vitruvius' wise words offer little help in our quest; until, that is, we discover how the three features required are related to each other. We shall see, and we shall need to assess, what rides on the fact that architecture is essentially functional. We must face up to the view that exhibiting utility has had architecture black-balled from membership of the brotherhood of fine arts. There is something grubby about utility, or so it is thought in some circles. The noble arts are too refined, some would say, for association with utility. (Illustration is besmirched by the same dogma. Since illustration is constrained by the depiction of a set text or narrative, its pictures are deemed inferior to the fine art of painting in which the artist is free to paint what she likes.) The view that architecture is a fine art must contend with this conceit, and it will.

So, the problem at the centre of our ruminations in this book shall be the status of architecture as a fine art. There is opposition. When Hannes Meyer, the Swiss architect, became the second director of the Bauhaus Dessau, from 1928 to 1930, he renamed what was 'The Department of Architecture' as 'The Department of Building', quite reasonably interpreted as putting forward utility and strength over beauty, and hence rejoicing in the relegation of architecture to building.

Returning to Alberti, Eck turns our attention away from regarding classicism as his model and puts in its place nature. Thus, he can admire and be influenced by classicism, even whilst, *through* his admiration for its examples, he regards nature as the original source of all that is beautiful and the source of his inspiration. After regarding the kings of Asia, who built large-scale buildings as a result of, and as a testament to, their great wealth, Alberti turns to the Greeks, who began to search for perfection in the arts: that which can only be altered to its detriment. It is here that architecture begins to compete with wealth, so that artistic beauty outshines ostentation.

Here is Alberti nailing several colours to the mast,

> The Greeks therefore decided that it was their part to surpass through ingenuity those whose wealth they could not rival, in whatever work they undertook. As with other arts, so with building, they sought it in, and drew it out from, the very bosom of Nature, and began to discuss and examine it thoroughly, studying and weighing it up with great incisiveness and subtlety.
> (Alberti 1988, 157–8)

Alberti's conception of the architect as fine artist is prescient. Our considerations of architecture as an art are at least compatible with some of what he has to tell us. He certainly considers it one of the 'noble arts' and sets this out in the prologue, where he writes within the opening paragraph that 'All of [the arts] seem to compete toward the one end, to be the greatest possible use to humanity, yet we realize that each has some integral property, which shows it has a different advantage to offer from the others.'

This presages eighteenth-century developments of aesthetics and the system of the arts remarked upon by Kristeller. Eck develops her theme, citing Alberti's conception of the architect and the nature of the subject in which she is engaged. She discusses three elements of the art undertaken. These are, according to Alberti, '*lineamenta*', '*materia*' and '*opus*' (lineaments, material and work). In their glossary, the translators use 'lineaments', 'line', 'linear characteristics' and 'design' for '*lineamenta*'. What Alberti makes clear in his prologue is that lineaments are of a different order than material.

> The whole form and appearance of the building may depend on lineaments alone. Nor do lineaments have anything to do with material (...) It is quite possible to project whole forms in the mind without any recourse to the material, by designating and determining a fixed orientation and conjunction for the various angles. Since that is the case, let lineaments be the precise and correct outline, conceived in the mind, made up of lines and angles, and perfected in the learned intellect and imagination.
> (Alberti 1988, 7)

A-historical: this is. For it is of a piece with contemporary thinking that the material is worked by the craftsman (Alberti's 'carpenter') according to the design (*lineamenta*). The architect is in no unique position among the arts; for music and dance, the composer and choreographer, respectively, take responsibility for that which will be performed by the orchestra and the dance troop. Slightly modifying his claim, and for the good, Alberti acknowledges that the act of designing depends upon the imagination and its delivery in the drawings; and then further, the delivery of the drawings in the model, where each follows from the other as a matter of course. The continuum of this exercise of design, from imagination through drawing into the model is to be adjusted at each of its stages,

> But I can say this of myself: I have often conceived of projects in the mind that seemed quite commendable at the time; but when I translated them into drawings, I found several errors in the very parts that delighted me most, and quite serious ones; again, when I return to drawings, and measure the dimensions, I recognize and lament my carelessness; finally, when I pass from

> the drawings to the model, I sometimes notice further mistakes in the individual parts.
>
> (Alberti 1988, 317)

It is here that Alberti recognizes the critical dimension of any art practice; that there is a sort of discourse between the work of the artist and the medium within which she works. So that we can see the imagination alive in the process of becoming an organized piece of work. It is not until the drawings are made that the angles are seen to be 'too sharp', 'too oblique', the parallel lines 'too narrow', 'too wide'; and then when these have been adjusted accordingly, when the architect proceeds to her model, the spaces are 'too cramped', 'too vacant' the details 'too heavy', 'too flimsy'. It is interesting that Alberti also prizes the model as the best image of the projected work. For it is here that he suggests the imagination of the client is best engaged.

VI Fine art-kinds, medium specificity, and 'the buck passing theory'

Whilst, mid-twentieth century, Kristeller searched for an eighteenth-century system, we might remind ourselves that as for the first part of the twentieth century (at least) contemporary artists and their critics sought to do away with the classification of the arts into the various kinds with which we are, nevertheless, familiar. Modernism, at least in some of its numerous versions, regarded art simpliciter as a legitimate aim, even going so far as to see the freedom from particularity as artistic liberation. (We saw a version of this view when we considered Womersley's *High Sunderland* and Kjærholm's *PK25* in Chapter 1.) By art-kinds, I follow Lopes whose 'buck passing' theory demands that we provide, for each art-kind, an essential characteristic by which we identify it (Lopes 2014). We are used to Duchamp's 'readymades'; the art works that provoked argument about what possible strictures might be instituted to legislate the forms that art should take. In doing so, Duchamp inaugurates and exploits the move away from given formal constraint to an attitude taken up by the artist and then encountered by the spectator.

The spectator, under Duchamp's revision, has to enter into the attitude the artist strikes up. Duchamp calls for 'an art of the mind', having had enough of 'art of the hand'. By exhibiting his readymades Duchamp, in effect, claimed that anything can be art, and the avant-garde celebrated this freedom and trundled happily along beneath his banner. The viewer must either confront the work or surrender to its cleverness. Even if beauty evaporates in this hothouse, the encounter might be enjoyable, potentially, as a contemporary conversation on the possibilities of art. (Whilst not considering conversations as fine art, Kant does count them as 'agreeable arts', and gives good account of what it is to have an enjoyable evening meal with guests.) That said, aesthetics and fine art look to have taken, at least temporarily, a seat at the back.

Lopes looks at what he calls 'the hard cases'; that plethora of avant-garde art works that succeeded the readymades. To these he proposes a spirited answer to a moribund question: 'But is it art?'

Lopes' theory claims there is no unified system of the arts. And so there is nothing external to the art-kind that can explain why its objects are works of fine art. Its being a work of fine art depends upon nothing other than its belonging to the particular art-kind. Art is just painting and sculpture and dance and film and architecture, etc.

What motivates his theory is the *impasse* we have reached in aesthetics in dealing with the hard cases. What he calls the 'hard cases' are works by artists that defy the definitions of art that have been held central. So, notoriously, Duchamp's *Fountain* has been used as the standard model – the DaDa movement's anti-rational procedures stand as the first occasion of works that were meant to *disregard* tradition rather than revise or subvert or reinterpret. The twentieth-century *avant-garde* is then littered with works that fly in the face of any philosophical definition of art. The new art became philosophical, its works designed to combat any purported definition philosophers might propose. Hence the brilliance of George Dickie and then Arthur Danto with their various versions of the Institutional Theory. The institutional theories variously posit that *x* is a work of art if *x* has bestowed upon it the status of a work of art by all or most of the 'Artworld' – or by a specified person with institutional authority.

Lopes does not let himself off lightly. He picks up a yet more problematic case than *Fountain*. He chooses as his example, Robert

Barry's *Inert Gas Series/Helium, Neon, Argon, Krypton, Xenon/ From a Measured Volume to Indefinite Expansion* (1969). The work isn't perceptible. Its only form, exhibited in the galleries and collected by wealthy moderns, is the documented evidence of the release of the various gases. And so, with this in mind we have now to locate the work. It is in the face of these questions – 'What is the work?' and, when we settle upon its identity, 'Is it a work of art?' – that we find ourselves spinning vertiginously out of control.

What better explains the hard cases is Lopes' buck passing theory. We must ask: if Barry's *Inert Gas Series* is a work of art, then, when it comes to passing the buck, to what art-kind does it belong? According to Lopes, it is a feature of art-kinds that they have media profiles. Paintings are not just made of paint. They are made in the medium of paint. Arguably, that medium constrains paintings to have representational properties, and the exploitation of the medium to render representational effects calls upon the spectator to see not only the represented world but the way the medium is exploited to bring about that depicted world (Wollheim 1987). So, if Barry's gas works are works of art, they do not belong to the art-kind painting. Similarly, they do not belong to music, poetry, architecture, dance, sculpture and so on. Then what are they? Now, just as art-kinds can die, so new art-kinds can be brought into existence.

The art of illuminating manuscripts is all but dead. By contrast, photography, video, film, installation, performance art, sound art and so on are relative newcomers, recently emerged and presently thriving.

So, when we encounter a putative work such as *Fountain*, we must ask, to what art-kind does this belong? In the absence of a candidate art-kind, it looks as if we are faced with the problem of either withdrawing its art status or conceding its 'free agent' status. That is, either *Fountain* is not a work of art or it is a work of art that belongs to no art-kind: a free agent. Lopes' ingenious strategy is to remind us of the newness of many art-kinds. One way to deal with *Fountain* is to consider it as a prototypical work in a new medium profile. Exhibited in 1917, the work has now become embedded within the art-kind, Conceptual Art, a movement that had its heyday in the 1960s and 1970s. Thus, Fountain becomes prototypical of the hard cases. Time has told that *Fountain* belongs within that body of work – specifically as a prototype.

Lopes' view, developed in this highly original work, has very wide implications for the convergence of the philosophy of art, art criticism and art practice, alongside other disciplines such as anthropology, literary theory, art theory and empirical studies such as psychology and sociology.

The new concept of fine art, introduced by Baumgarten and developed by Kant, recognized the disparity of the fine arts and the properties that each art had independently of the others – that painting is a (relatively) flat expanse of colour representing a three-dimensional world together with things, scenes and events therein; that music is made of sounds organized through succession in time according to a tonal structure, for example. The unity of the arts, therefore, stepped back from the objects themselves and sought to explain our attitude to them as a peculiar facet of mind. The fine arts comprise those *works* that engage this attitude and, through it, provide us with a certain kind of pleasure.

Lopes' recent book is focused on Conceptualism, attempting to rescue it from the clutches of the much-criticized institutional theory's *ad hoc* design to accommodate it (Lopes 2014). In it, *pace* the institutional theory, he defends the view that all works of art belong to an art-kind. Mimesis provided these pursuits with a certain status in antiquity – a status that attributed to them skills, each with a role in cognition. Through the deployment of these skills by poets, dramatists, painters or sculptors, we were supposed to be able to access certain aspects of the world. Music enabled us to see more clearly character as that was expressed in movement. Architecture, it was claimed, provided access to images of our preliminary conquest of nature in the building of our primitive homes. Having reviewed the mimetic view of fine art, and found it inadequate, we must now try to identify the defining strictures of architecture as a fine art.

By requiring each of the individual arts to be identified and accorded its own parameters, Lopes anchors our understanding of works of art to the medium in which they are fashioned. Our understanding, thus anchored, proscribes unsecured works that would otherwise float freely upon the tides of art. There are no 'free agents', no such flotsam. He tells us:

> The buck passing theory is correct if it is viable and more informative than its competition. It is more informative than its

> competition if it is no less systematically informative, if it better grounds empirical art studies, if it better grounds art criticism, and if it deals more effectively with the hard cases. It is viable if it answers (...) the free agent objection. While it is no less systematically informative than buck stopping theories, it better grounds empirical art studies and art criticism, and it answers the (...) free agent objection. Most importantly, it deals more effectively with the hard cases than does its competition. Ergo, the buck passing theory of art is correct.
>
> (Lopes 2014, 22–3)

It is a deficiency of the institutional theory that its one apparent virtue, its *carte blanche* promiscuity, licenses just anything (and everything) to be a work of art. (Ed Kienholz made a title plaque, *The World*, which he then attached to the world, hence claiming the world to be an Ed & Nancy Keinholz 'readymade'.) Having established that anything can be a work of art, it lacks the critical resources to say why one thing, rather than another, is elected to such status. We can still ask, *Why* has the institution declared this a work of art? Wollheim asks this in his essay critical of the institutional theory (Wollheim 2012). Whereas the theory that each work belongs to an art-kind brings with it a tradition in which the teaching of an art's practice and the criticism of works within that practice follows as a matter of course.

That our interest in art is aesthetic is explicable in these terms. We ask, 'What is a work of art?' and we are told it is a work made with the intention to afford a particular kind of aesthetic experience. It provides us with an experience of adherent beauty through which we can grasp certain sorts of ideas. That answer does not thereby define what art is; it merely 'passes the buck' to each of the individual arts to explain how our engagement with the medium of *that* practice, with *its* traditions and concomitant expectations, furnishes such peculiar experiences. I cannot move from the particular aesthetic appreciation appropriate to painting (through my understanding of *its* medium), to an aesthetic appreciation of music, without first (and independently) coming to an understanding of the medium of music. Nothing about my proficiency in confidently grasping painting as an art will thereby furnish me with an appropriate level of expertise in music. Hence, 'the buck passing theory'.

VII The coffee mug objection and conceptualism

Lopes places demands upon theories of the arts. If there is a medium of ceramic art, we must be able to say how it is that Grayson Perry's *Rosetta Vase* is a work of art, whilst my coffee mug is not. We need a concept of medium that can allow the one to be a work of art in the medium of ceramics whilst the other remains a mere piece of the world, albeit a crafted ceramic piece of the world. Lopes identifies this as the 'coffee mug objection'. To answer the coffee mug objection we have to say more about the medium than that it is to be identified with mere stuff. There is a difference between Nicolas Poussin's *A Dance to the Music of Time*, and a depiction of a wanted man nailed outside the swinging doors of a wild-west saloon. The former is, whilst the latter is not, a work of art. Wollheim's notion of a medium is sensitive to this.

Wollheim does not think that just anything made with coloured paint is a painting. The material is not the medium. Lopes agrees. He writes that the ceramic slip used by manufacturers of coffee mugs is the same slip used by ceramic artists. The stuffs are the same in each case. Then what makes a painting and a ceramic piece, each the work of Picasso, works of art – whilst a painted scene illustrating courtroom proceedings and a coffee mug are not? The view is that in the former, but not the latter cases, the material is recruited to a medium. (Lopes calls this a medium profile.) It is the medium profile (for any art) that prescribes the nature of 'belonging' to which any work must conform.

Lopes has to argue that Conceptualism has the resources of an art-kind; that there is a medium it exploits. In so saying, he calls upon the non-material aspects of the medium of conceptual art but maintains that such non-material features of the art are nevertheless acceptable as features of a medium; that they suffice to establish a medium profile. Duchamp's bottle rack and snow shovel, along with all the other readymades, are then recruited retrospectively as prototypical works of Conceptual art. New art-kinds are permitted just so long as we find them capable of sustaining the medium that develops around them. Traditions start somewhere. Why not here? Performance art is not theatre. Installation art is not sculpture. Photography is not painting. Yet each of these arts can be said to have

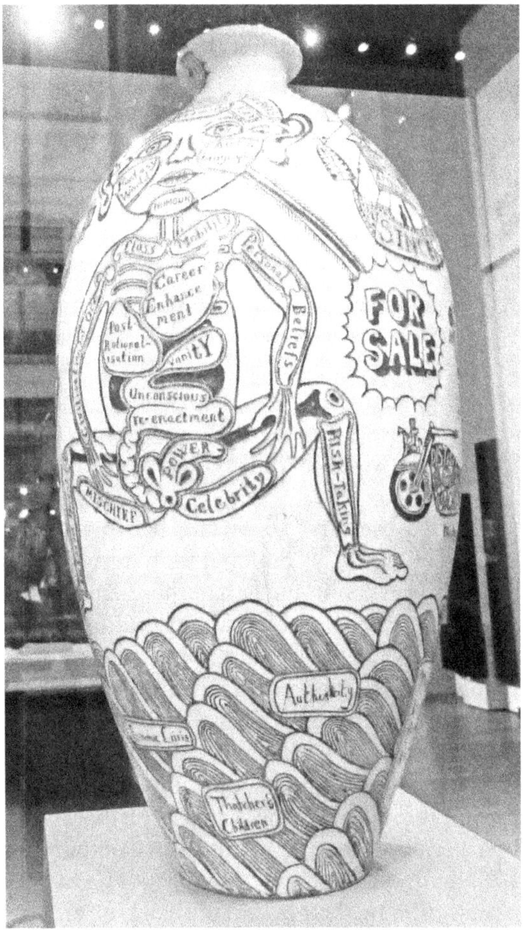

FIGURE 3.3 *Grayson Perry,* Rosetta Vase, *2011. © amandabhslater, 2021.*

relations with the established art mentioned. We find our feet in the new media because we know where we stand with the established media with which we are able to compare them. Conceptual art is developed out of the visual arts and is particularly clarified when seen against the backdrop of Greenberg's Modernism.

(Greenberg's formalist aesthetic permitted no narrative content as aesthetically relevant; and so moral and political preoccupations were banished from the aesthetics of painting at a stroke. Aesthetics became a matter of exquisite pleasure in the mere form of the object at which one gazed. It is for this reason that the conceptualists abandoned the search for such beauty in art. Greenberg had made it simultaneously elitist and socially irrelevant.)

One strand of modernist architecture reacted against functionalists like Meyer, seeking instead an architecture based on its own internal geometric demands. In this endeavour, we can see how the artistic concerns of some modernist abstract painting and sculpture attempt to cross boundaries and make for a conception of architecture, constrained by theory predominating in the cousinhood of the visual fine arts. Womersley is an example we have considered, but so too is the architect and theoretician, Peter Eisenman.

Eisenman coined the term, to locate his own work, as 'Post-functionalism'. Claiming the building as a result of process and as a record of it, he maintained that the elements must not be subordinated to prescribed functions but should be freely articulate as a geometry. The result of such a view can be seen in *House VI*, whose play of forms prohibits the bedroom accommodating a double bed. A glass partition divides the room and the occupants must sleep either side of it in single beds. There is an upside-down staircase and there are columns offering no structural support but which abut the table in the kitchen further prohibiting the communal gathering around it for meals. (Compare and contrast this with Langlands' & Bell's *Eclipse*, fig. 1.1) This is, clearly, an ostentatious rejection of the idea that a work of architecture must address function. Eisenman addresses function, but in such a way that it is deliberately rejected. Post-functionalism has functionalism in its sights, and in this way he can claim to be working within the confines of the art-kind. Or can he? Is this a parallel attempt by architecture, in concert with the conceptualists, to liberate art from the constraints set upon it as an individual art-kind?

As we have noted, part of the assumptions and expectations against which conceptual artists mutinied was a certain form of aesthetics propounded by Greenberg. It is within the medium of painting that the scene is set for the new art. Moreover, given Greenberg's formalist aesthetics, it is understandable that

FIGURE 3.4 *Peter Eisenman,* House VI, *1975. © G.oorthuys, 1977.*

conceptualists regard Duchamp's readymades as prototypical works in an art-kind around which they sought to make sense of their new work.

A pertinent worry, however, is that Duchamp claimed the readymades were chosen precisely because they had no aesthetic qualities:

> A POINT WHICH I WANT VERY MUCH TO ESTABLISH IS THAT THE CHOICE OF THESE 'READYMADES' WAS NEVER DICTATED BY ESTHETIC DELECTATION.
>
> THIS CHOICE WAS BASED ON A REACTION OF VISUAL INDIFFERENCE WITH AT THE SAME TIME A TOTAL ABSENCE OF GOOD OR BAD TASTE (...) IN FACT A COMPLETE ANESTHESIA.
>
> (Duchamp 1975, 141)

(That's a bit 'shouty', but it is very much within the tradition of artists' statements and their endeavours at more formal manifestos.)

In this case there is undoubtedly a visual experience of the work, but Duchamp claims that it is aesthetically indifferent with respect to its visual phenomenology. On painting, Duchamp has said, 'painting should not be exclusively retinal or visual, it should have to do with grey matter, with our urge for understanding' (Duchamp 1975, 136). His turning against the 'exclusively retinal or visual' is surely what the conceptual artists were doing when they rebelled against Greenberg. What Wollheim has had to say about painting is enough to support the view that no painting is exclusively retinal but that painting as an art *is* exclusively visual. That is no contradiction. But if Duchamp's work can be seen to advantage as a prototypical conceptualist work in a medium which is not necessarily visual, then we must wait upon critical and historical evaluation to pass judgement.

Can we see *House VI* as a piece of conceptual art, unconstrained by the medium dictates of architecture as an art-kind? What happens when you release works of art from their familiar surroundings? It shares with the readymades a disavowal of the aesthetic as that is regarded in perceptual terms. For at no point does Eisenman call upon judgements of beauty in support of his work. Like the conceptualists, he is concerned more with meaning than with pleasure. Yet, *House VI* was commissioned by the Franks. Suzanne Frank has written on the house and claims that the family loves living in such a poetic structure. Whether poetry can be seen as a motive for Eisenman, we must again refer to the critics.

If *House VI* is not to be considered architecture, it must stand or fall as a work of conceptualism. In excluding the ceramic mug from the art-kind ceramics, we needed to show that Perry's *Rosetta Vase* belonged to the art-kind by exploiting the medium of ceramics, and by showing that the coffee mug did not belong because no attempt was made to make a work of art.

Is Eisenman making a work of architecture or is he making a work within the art-kind Conceptualism? It seems he is caught upon the horns of a dilemma – if, that is, we abide by the buck passing theory. However, it is useful for us to consider the question, even if he might reject the theory to which we adhere. For it focuses attention on what it was that he was doing when he drew up his preparations to build – drawings, models, grid schemes, geometrical arrangements and so on. Recall the prescience of Wollheim's remark, 'The truth is that Verdi composed his operas under the concept "opera"'. That concept, the buck passing theory tells us is regulative in that it prescribes the medium specification of the work under view.

The buck passing theory's medium specificity is coterminous with Wollheim's conception of what he called the 'artist's theory'. (Note that for Wollheim, an artist has to work under the regulation of a theory. However, it is not a precondition of an artist working under a theory that she should know what that theory is. The buck passing theory, likewise, presents Duchamp's readymades as prototypically conceptual art, even though that medium was yet to have emerged as a theory of the kind of art Duchamp was making.)

So, in both Wollheim and Lopes we find a ground for discussing the artist's intention. The artist, like her non-artist counterpart, can act intentionally without having her intentions present to mind. Indeed, in both the artist and non-artist cases, there may be good reason to think that on occasion she may resist acknowledgement of the intentions which characterize her actions. She might, in good conscience, disavow the attributed intentions, whilst yet acting under their regulation.

House VI is a work of architecture if we can adumbrate a medium-specific account of architecture into which it fits. It fails *to be* a work of architecture just if, having arrived at an account of architecture's medium specificity, we cannot so place it.

Wollheim provides such a case for the medium specificity of painting. The medium of painting is such that the materials of the painter are mobilized towards representational ends. In this respect, Wollheim demonstrates the limits of painting as a medium and thereby establishes the relationship between what the contemporary painter is at liberty to make within the medium confines and what the history of painting has so far comprised.

It is for this reason that we were able to regard the images of cave dwellers as picture making, but not as painting. For the medium of painting had not arrived during the periods in which images were made on the interior walls of caves. (Nothing in the cave persuades us that the configuration of the image is exploited in such a way that we should include it in a complex twofold experience.)

At last, we can see that the vexed relationship between dwelling and architecture can be established as that between a pre-disposition to shelter and protect ourselves, on the one hand, and a cultural embodiment of this pre-disposition in the fine art of architecture.

Before we develop that medium specificity for architecture – and before we answer the demanding question concerning *House VI* – we must say more about the frontier between fine art and non-art craft works or artefacts.

VIII Appreciative kinds and their reach

Lopes introduces the notion of an 'appreciative kind', and this ought to help us with our consideration of those things we appreciate but which we do not consider works of art. So, according to Lopes, the range of appreciative kinds is broader in spectrum than is the collection of the individual arts, which it nevertheless includes. Moreover, by attending to appreciative kinds we can compare individual art-kinds with other art-kinds, as when we compare the novel with verse, intaglio printing with drawing, drawing with painting and with sculpture. But we can also compare appreciative kinds where one of the kinds is a fine art and the other is not. We can, for instance, compare dance with ice-dance, the novel with biography, architecture with building. Appreciative kinds, that is, permit us to move from our understanding and appreciation of the arts across to our appreciation of non-arts, and we can have an aesthetic appreciation of the latter as well as the former. A warning note, however,

> Yuriko Saito has argued passionately for an expansion of our interest beyond the arts to include the stuff of everyday life, which is 'a treasure trove of materials for investigation'.
>
> Some worry that the strategy is dangerous (…) The minute it makes sense to compare something to art, it is tempting to treat it as art. The danger is that it denatures the stuff of everyday life to treat it as art.
>
> (Lopes 2014, 121)

The warning is particularly apposite to architecture. Chapter 1 should have warned us that treating architecture as dwelling *de-natures* dwelling. That is not what architecture is. We concluded that chapter by insisting that architecture emerges from, but cannot be reduced to, our natural pre-disposition to find our home and to accommodate our *natural* lives.

Nevertheless, we can be clearer about what is at stake in attending to art-kinds on the one hand and non-art appreciative kinds on the other. Art-kinds require attention to their constitutive media. Lacking any such media, appreciative kinds, beyond art, are to be attended to, appreciated, outwith the conjoined restrictions and permissions afforded by any such specified media.

However, a corollary of this conclusion is that appreciative kinds beyond the individual arts stand in need of explanation that cannot rely upon medium explication. The various fine art media were identified as the correlative bases for aesthetic appreciation in the arts. If a non-art practice could be provided with a medium description sufficient to require its products to be aesthetically appreciated, under the constraint of that medium, that practice should be, thereby, considered a candidate for art-kind status. (It might well be that ice-dance is promoted to art-kind status, or that it is sufficiently developed to be included within the art-kind, dance, just as are polka, the cha-cha and the merengue.)

IX Architecture and the everyday

Kant individuated the arts, each of which had its own character and rank, with poetry at its highest. If anything unified the individual arts it was that each had the capacity to promote genius. Genius belonged only to the arts. The brilliance of scientists, philosophers, footballers and statesmen was to be acknowledged as a different kind of achievement. The mark of genius is originality – a feature unrequired by science, philosophy, sport and politics. The genius makes a work that exhibits originality but that looks natural – as if second nature to the artist, effortless. The work of genius sets a standard for others to follow – a rule which itself follows no rule. We can only marvel at such works, as can the artists themselves, for not even they know how the work originated. Kant, however, thinks that whatever the rule introduced by the artist, it legislates practice within that art-kind.

Within the individual arts, the genius works her medium to effect. Each art permits the formulation within it of an 'aesthetic idea'. Aesthetic ideas quicken the mind. An aesthetic idea is a presentation that cannot be formulated using concepts of cognition, or else we could exhaustively spell out the meaning of a work and its beauty would evaporate.

For Kant, the fine arts are a means of communicating aesthetic ideas. There can be no adequate conceptual content that will suffice to capture what it is that is given in a work of fine art. The work will always outstretch the conceptual content provided by any description. Then, in what way is it communicative? It is symbolic, and in this sense the symbol is allegoric. So that, for Kant, we can have aesthetic ideas of death, love and envy presented in allegoric form. We have already considered examples of symbolism in architecture. We drew upon the scene from *Witness*, in which the community comes together to make a barn, the building symbolic of the body of a community. We also saw how Muñoz Molina regarded the School of Philosophy and Letters as a symbol of the community of humanities and arts.

And so, in considering the fine arts, generally, we must look for their success in communicating aesthetic ideas in such a way that our minds are enlivened by a work's ability to demonstrate a feeling appropriate to the matter communicated. And in this we grasp the rule by which a work can be measured. Our minds are 'quickened' by the work.

Without contesting this claim for the arts in general, Roger Scruton has called into question its place in a theory of architecture.

> [It is not] tenable to think of architecture as a 'fine art' on a par with other forms of intimate expression, directed at those with an ear or an eye for their particular product. The aesthetic constraints on architecture, I argue, are part of an 'aesthetics of everyday life' which makes demands that are to a large extent independent of personal tastes and individual expressive aims.
>
> (Scruton 2012, 298)

On this account, Scruton tells us that if the individual arts are conceived as appreciative kinds, characterized by their individual media evolved to foster brilliance in the expression of genius, then architecture is an appreciative kind that relinquishes the need for such brilliance; it seeks not to foster new and original experience, and, presumably, eschews the medium specificity that encourages it. Scruton, so to speak, relegates architecture. Rather than grant architects the status of 'fine artist', they should be regarded as journeymen, able to direct the building of municipal works in accordance with pattern books passed down through the ages – just as the law is bequeathed from one generation to the next. So, architecture is an art that requires no genius, for the purpose of architecture is communal and homely – requiring no novel experiences but rather preserving the conditions under which our feeling at home can be comfortably framed. Scruton writes of an 'aesthetics of everyday life' but in fact he identifies architecture as an everyday art. Other everyday arts might include storytelling, jokes, amateur photography, biography, travelogue and memoir – all of which are capable of presenting their audience with aesthetic experiences, if not aesthetic ideas. Perhaps it's the mark of an everyday art that it should have this profile, whilst lacking a medium.

The idea of home, of well-observed manners and of settlement, all get to fund the idea of a communal art. (We have already considered Kant's view of the dinner conversation as an agreeable art.) Unlike nature, such an art is entered into and not merely contemplated. We find ourselves at home in architecture; indeed, we make ourselves at home in it. Scruton has written on beauty and uses the meal as an image of such a project. Here he considers the hostess laying a table,

> The jug alludes to a certain form of life: the Mediterranean life in which rough wine is in plentiful supply, and in frictionless relation to both work and play. That is why the hostess chose a jug of naively decorated earthenware, and why she put it in the middle of the table, signifying the easy-going use of it in which we help ourselves. These may not be conscious choices.
>
> (Scruton 2009, 92)

It is a feature of aesthetics, as I have sought to describe it, that it is captured by phenomenological descriptions. There is always 'something it is like' to undergo aesthetic experience. In seeking aesthetic experience, we want those experiences that are richer than merely perceiving the world. We want, in our experiences, our imaginations to be engaged. In her book, *At the Existentialist Café*, Sarah Bakewell writes of Heidegger's conception of human life as being like the creation of a clearing in a forest, where we can become ourselves and let other beings emerge into that clearing to be themselves, to 'unhide' themselves. And she tells us,

> Death, [Wollheim] wrote, is the great enemy not merely because it deprives us of all the future things we might do, and all the pleasures we might experience. It takes away the ability to experience anything at all, ever. It puts an end to our being a Heideggerian clearing of things to emerge into. Thus, as Wollheim says, 'It deprives us of phenomenology, and, once having tasted phenomenology, we develop a longing for it which we cannot give up.' Having had experience of the world, having had intentionality, we want to continue it forever, because that experience of the world is what we are.
>
> Unfortunately, this is the deal we get. We can taste phenomenology only because, one day, it will be taken from us. We clear our space, then the forest reclaims it again. The only consolation is to have had the beauty of seeing light through the leaves at all: to have had something, rather than nothing.
>
> (Bakewell 2016, 299–300)

The clearing in the forest is a Heideggerian image. It represents an uncovering. It becomes a place in which we come to see other creatures than ourselves; and in this clearing, and in the seeing of others, we also come to see ourselves. Then, as time passes, the clearing again becomes overgrown. There is a mythical sense to this image, itself a form of symbol. It is Heidegger in his poetic phase. What this image shows is that our work, *real work*, is this uncovering, that needs to be undertaken by each generation in succession.

Everyday aesthetics looks as if it has soft if not permeable borders along its frontier with the fine arts. However, the appearance of easy migration between the two constituencies ought to encourage us to look for the aesthetic in all areas of life – as artists do when furnishing their homes. We snoop around the homes of artists, now bequeathed as visitor centres or museums, and we notice how finely these artists have chosen the objects that make up the environment in which they lived and worked. Their furniture and their kitchen utensils take on a significance for having been chosen by them. So that it's easy to see how those involved in the fine arts are given to the aesthetics of the everyday. Moreover, it is easy to see how an involvement with making art should spread its outlook upon the way we live.

> It seems to me natural to think that art is more deeply rooted in human nature than morality, and I am surprised that philosophers make little of the fact that, though good art is more likeable than bad art, virtuous people do not enjoy this same advantage over those to whom we are drawn primarily for their charm, or their gaiety, or their sweetness of nature, or their outrageousness.
>
> (Wollheim 1993, x)

Wollheim writes of the privilege aesthetics enjoys in comparison to the world of morality. The warm charm of the aesthetic trumps the cold glare of the moral gaze. But what does it mean for aesthetics to be more deeply rooted in human nature?

4

Imagination and combobulation

I Aristotle and Hume

Architects, with justification, speak and write about the nature of their work in space and time. Their work, after all, is generally considered to be concerned with the manipulation of lived space, so as to provide accommodation for our activities, all of which are enjoyed in terms of our spatial relations to the work and through our episodic experience of it. There is no one point of view upon a work. It is apprehended through a number of perceptions stitched together to reveal an agglomerated complex experience; made up of accumulated fragments and amalgamated into a whole relative to our purposes. Architecture is occupied by persons moving in and through the work, such that, even when temporarily resting in one place with one view, this is but a constituent experience of the larger complex apprehension. What are the contributions of space and time to architectural experience? In order to answer that question, we need to think about the nature of space and time in our general cognitive structure.

The production of the complex experience of architecture requires imagination. In this chapter we look at the nature and role of imagination as that is identified in the Western tradition of philosophy. In the next chapter, we shall move on to show how Kant's development of that conception of imagination is brought to bear upon *aesthetic* experience.

At least as far back as Aristotle we find a philosopher discussing imagination and weighing its contribution to our apprehension of the world. Here, in *De Anima* [*On the Soul*], is Aristotle on the distinction between sense (perceptual experience) and imagination,

> That imagination is not sense is clear from the following considerations: Sense is either a faculty or an activity, e.g. sight or seeing: imagination takes place in the absence of both, as e.g. in dreams. Again, sense is always present, imagination not. (...) [S]ensations are always true, imaginations are for the most part false. Once more, we do not, when sense functions precisely with regard to its object, say that we imagine it to be a man, but rather when there is some failure of accuracy in its exercise – then it is either true or false. And, as we were saying before, visions appear to us even when our eyes are shut. Neither is imagination any of the things that are never in error: e.g. knowledge or intelligence; for imagination may be false.
>
> (Aristotle 1984b, 427^{b} 28–428^{a} 18)

In *On Memory*, he writes again on the nature of sense as being in the presence of that which gives rise to veridical perception; in contrast to the need to recall what is absent from perception in memory. Perception, we are to conclude, is always a view upon the here and now.

In any dealing with what is not present, either its being thought up or its being recalled, we operate by directing our thoughts. Imagining a centaur or recalling the smile of an absent loved one involves agency. Whereas seeing the dog and hearing it bark, as it gazes up a tree at a squirrel is – at least pre-philosophically – passive.

Hume held that we could not discern an 'I' whose continuance guarantees a self. What evidence there is, shows only that there is a succession of bundles of sensations that impinge upon a subject, but this does not show that the subject itself endures through the changes in the sensations that so present themselves. Thus, Hume's scepticism raises a question concerning the self which, if left unattended, leads to the conclusion that we are, each of us, simply a variety of separate bundles of incoming sensation; and that we somehow *imagine* that these successive bundles belong to an enduring self.

In connection with this worry, Hume cannot, as it stands, account for the role that memory plays in our consciousness. For, if

I am nothing more than an awareness of present impressions, how do I recollect previous impressions and secure their place in the history of those impressions that, here and now, flood in upon me? In answer to this, Hume posits ideas. Derived from impressions, they are like impressions but lack their vivacity. Memory is the experience of ideas less vivid than the impressions from which they originate. Thus, memories are faded impressions. He contrasts memory with imagination. Ideas of imagination likewise have their source in impressions. However, these are much less vivid and they can be combined and arranged as when we think of a centaur – thereby combining our memory idea of a horse with that of a man.

In a similarly sceptical frame of mind, he argued that we could not derive a law of causality from the constant conjunction of events type, B, following immediately from events type, A. To recycle one of his examples: in billiards (or in snooker or pool) a cue ball strikes an object ball on its left-hand side, and this is constantly succeeded by the object ball moving off to the right. The direction is constantly predicted to be in a line that could be drawn between the centres of the two balls at the instant of their collision. However, Hume holds, this does not *prove* the cue ball caused the object ball to so move; any more than that night causes day, or day night; or that my wearing red socks causes it to rain – an unlikely but possible conjunction of successive events that might just happen to maintain its constancy. Luck, I suppose.

(We should remember the constancy with which we once observed swans and found them, each, to be white. The conclusion was reasonably arrived at that all swans are white. However, the observation of a black swan falsified that claim. There is nothing in the structure of being a swan that explains its being white.)

Hume's *empiricism* constrains him to seek the 'idea' of causation in observation. However, we do not, merely by observation, see causes. What we see is the persistent conjunction of event type, A, being followed immediately by event type, B. How then is Hume to set in place a foundation for our belief in, and reliance upon, causality?

On the nature of continuous experience, he calls upon imagination to glue each perception to the next as a collection of individual impressions received by the passive mind. Perception, as we have seen in the writing of Aristotle, provides the *here* and *now* of the impression. For Hume, however, as that passes in a mere instant it becomes a faded impression, much like a perception but less vivid. Nevertheless, its fading away whilst being replaced by the new 'here and now' provides the continuity of experience; and for Hume, this passage from the full impression to the fading impression to the faded impression is what gives us the *experience* of continuation in perception. Imagination is recruited to the task of providing the right kind of structure to the continuity of experience.

As for causality, Hume's scepticism raises the question of how it is that we can arrive at a belief in the nature of causality which posits a necessary connection between causes and their effects. Here, in the Treatise, is Hume's casting doubt on our common sense intuitions,

> To begin with the first question concerning the necessity of a cause: 'Tis a general maxim in philosophy, that *whatever begins to exist, must have a cause of existence*. This is commonly taken for granted in all reasonings, without any proof given or demanded. 'Tis suppos'd to be founded on intuition, and to be one of those maxims, which tho' they may be deny'd with the lips, 'tis impossible for men in their hearts really to doubt of. But if we examine this maxim by the idea of knowledge above-explain'd, we shall discover in it no mark of any such intuitive certainty; but on the contrary shall find, that 'tis of a nature quite foreign to that species of conviction.
>
> (Hume 1978, 78–9)

The 'idea of knowledge above-explain'd' is the empiricist account of all knowledge deriving from experience. Hume's answer to this set of problems, the upshot of the empiricist account by which he is inhibited, is to call upon our imagination.

Thus, Hume assigns a positive role of imagination to our daily experience of the world. However, its role merely closes the gap between seeming and being, in favour of seeming. Hume's scepticism remains unanswered if we simply rely upon the habit of exercising our imagination to lull us into believing in our continuous selves enjoying continuous experience of an orderly world obedient to the regulatory principle of causation.

What's more, Hume doesn't address Aristotle's observation that perception is different in kind from imagination. 'Faded impressions' (imaginings) are not impressions. They are at best recollected, but now absent, experiences of previously present impressions. What, then, gives warrant to recollection?

Aristotle is aware of this when, in *On Memory*, he writes,

> Now to remember what is future is not possible – that is an object of opinion or expectation (...); nor is there memory of what is present, but only sense perception. For by the latter we do not know what is future or past, but what is present only. But memory relates to what is past. No one would say that he remembers what is present, when it is present.
>
> (Aristotle 1984a, 449^{b} 10–15)

Thus, Aristotle regards sense perception as different in kind to memory, but he relates memory directly to imagination a little further on,

> [If] asked of which among the parts of the soul memory is a function, we reply: manifestly of that part to which imagination also appertains; and all objects of which there is imagination are in themselves objects of memory, while those objects which do not exist without imagination are objects of memory incidentally.
>
> (Aristotle 1984a, 450^{a} 21–25)

It is an act of recollection to have before our minds that which we once perceived: memories. Whilst objects which do not exist without imagination, a centaur for instance, is conjured up by conjoining images derived from memory. So, a centaur is composed of our memory image of a man conjoined with our memory image of a horse.

II Kant on space and time

Kant's *Critique of Pure Reason* (Kant 1964), published in German in 1781 and with a second amended edition in 1787, was the first of three *Critiques* and had, as its aim, the resolution of the discrepancy between rationalist and empiricist doctrines. (The first edition was published ten years after the concluding section of Book I of

Hume's *Treatise* appeared in German; a period coincident with Kant's 'decade of silence'; an interlude during which he continued to lecture but published nothing.)

Kant's transcendental idealism aimed to demonstrate that knowledge was neither exclusively based in *a priori* speculation (rationalism), nor entirely based on evidence accumulated through observation (empiricism). His solution is a synthesis of the two predominant philosophies of the age.

Between the two editions of the first *Critique*, he published *Prolegomena to Any Future Metaphysics*. In this book he recognizes Hume's contribution to 'Theoretical Philosophy', what we now call epistemology and metaphysics,

> *Hume* started mainly from a single but important concept in metaphysics, namely, that of the *connection of cause and effect* (and also its derivative concepts, of force and action, etc.), and called upon reason, which pretends to have generated this concept in her womb, to give him an account of by what right she thinks: that something could be so constituted that, if it is posited, something else necessarily must thereby also be posited; for that is what the concept of cause says. He indisputably proved that it is wholly impossible for reason to think such a connection *a priori* and from concepts, because the connection contains necessity; and it is simply not to be seen how it could be, that because something is, something else necessarily must also be, and therefore how the concept of such a connection could be produced *a priori*. From this he concluded that reason completely and fully deceives herself with this concept, falsely taking it for her own child, when it is nothing but a bastard of the imagination, which, impregnated by experience, and having brought certain representations under the law of association, passes off the resulting subjective necessity (i.e., habit) for an objective necessity (from insight). From which he concluded that reason has no power at all to think such connections, not even merely in general, because its concepts would then be bare fictions, and all of its cogitations allegedly established *a priori* would be nothing but falsely marked ordinary experiences; which is so much as to say that there is no metaphysics at all, and cannot be any.
>
> (Kant 2004, 7–8)

Kant sought to establish our knowledge of the world based upon the structure the mind must have if there is to be knowledge at all. He starts by establishing two *a priori* intuitions – conditions under which we must regard the objects of knowledge. The intuitions are time and space. Since space and time can be thought only as singularities, they do not fall under any such governing concept.

Kant's thought is this: if I am to think of a world, knowable to me, I must think of that world as both temporal and spatial. As things appear to me, they do so in a temporal order. Thus, events occur in succession, relative to each other; as before, now (fleetingly) and after. Objects must also be related to each other spatially in the outer world.

Time and space are not objects of thought. Rather, they are the conditions under which thought unfolds. They provide governance for thought, for its regulation. Time and space are not concepts, since concepts gather together instances of kinds. 'Dog', 'dyptheria', 'doormat' and 'dementia' are each concepts prevailing over the collection of instances of some kind. 'Dog' organizes examples of animals belonging to a defined class of four-legged mammals; the creature barking in the night is a dog. The creature in my living room chewing a bone is a dog. 'All dogs hate cats' makes a general claim about the nature of a dog and so on. To be a dog is to meet certain conceptual criteria. 'Dyptheria' is the concept of a serious infection caused by strains of bacteria called Corynebacterium diphtheriae. The bacteria are identified under a microscope according to certain observable features, or by chemical analysis in the laboratory. 'Doormats' are collected under a functional concept; that is, as a kind according to the functions for which they have been designed; a rough fabric patch of floor protection upon which to wipe footwear clean at the entrance to a building. Dementia, as its name suggests, is the unminding of persons, usually due to degeneration of the brain in old age. It is identified by diagnosis and by observation of a persistent collection of indicative symptoms. In each case, we are able to identify, as a uniting principle, the relevant concept under which the particular object of thought belongs.

But space and time are not classes of object and so do not have particular instances; they do not belong to kinds. Neither space nor time, therefore, falls under unifying concepts. Rather, they are the preconditions under which the *a priori* concepts, Kant's categories, are implemented. Space provides the possibility of thought about relations between substances (of which, e.g., things, of which e.g., artefacts, of which, e.g., pens). Time provides the possibility of thought about the relations between events, as one tumbles from another, and so determines the next (of which, e.g., causation, of which, e.g., action, of which, e.g., mark-making, of which, e.g., writing).

So, space and time, being part of the framework of thought, do not belong within it. We cannot, therefore, coherently 'think of' time and space. For, to attempt it, is to treat of the preconditions of thought as if they are its content. It is a mistake to think of space as a vast container. Space cannot be seen as a container without immediately thinking of it as having a boundary. So to see it, however, is to consider it as having an exterior, which is incoherent – as if space itself could be contained. Similarly, Kant suggests in the 'Antinomies' that were we to ask if time had a beginning, we would be drawn to two opposite conclusions, both of which seem necessarily true. It must have a beginning, he argues, or else an infinity of time would have already elapsed, but it is impossible for an infinity to be completed. It cannot have a beginning, he argues, otherwise there would have to be a point at which it began; and then we could properly ask, what happened before *that* time. Hence, Kant argues in this and the other antinomies that we should not extend reason beyond the scope of possible experience.

Having set up this basic structure, he proceeds to provide us with a series of concepts that we are to understand as necessary to the task of thinking at all. These concepts, 'The Categories', each mutually supports the other. So, for instance, the concept of *substance* contains within it the concept of something sustaining itself through time. Substance is that which remains the same through change. It is the enduring presence of a thing as its properties change. The red, ripe tomato is the same tomato as was once green. What endures through a change of mind, we might say, is the mind of the person whose view upon the world is transformed. Such self-sustenance entails causality, and thus we move from substance to causality by *a priori* reflection.

Once the categories are established *a priori*, we work down into them providing contingent empirical concepts as befits our *lifeworld*. In Chapter 2, we briefly considered the categories as they have been linked with Jung's work on archetypes, those which some have thought were in some way equivalent to the categories. We argued in that respect that Jung's archetypes might better be thought predispositions – the ways in which rational persons might be drawn, by their shared psychology, to mythologize aspects of the world to which science has not or could not minister. However, those dispositions, whilst possibly shared across humanity, are not the same as the categories as they are drawn down into Kant's scheme of cognition.

For Kant, the very possibility of thought, *in general*, depends upon conditions that must obtain; whereas for Jung, it is the condition of the *Lebenswelt* that calls upon us to posit mythological accounts of a magical realm. In Jung, mythology is called upon to fill in the gaps; and, due to our human condition, those gaps appear across the multi-cultural divide. For Kant there could be no thought at all, without the structure of mind he builds across humanity and logically prior to any cultural relativism.

Jung's archetypal thinking is not *a priori*. It is the tendency we have to explain that for which we have no explanation, in terms that we *already possess*. Thus, we see disaster as the result of agency; and, further, we posit an agent (or agents) responsible. These agents, even when they have animalistic features, are nevertheless human in terms of their agency and their motives. Moreover, it matters not that we *know* that these archetypal narratives are not true. They are symbols. Thus, they provide us with the kind of ideas Kant identified as the business of the fine arts. Our God, and the gods of other religions, are rich ideas given to us in order to make the world our own.

We have been considering myth as an outmoded unscientific account of what can be better dealt with by advances in science. Thus, we have thought myth somehow beneath our superior epistemic powers. The enlightenment has brought illumination to the dark parts of the world in which we previously cowered. This is not quite true.

Here, for instance, is Socrates in conversation with Phædrus concerning contemporary myth:

> *Phædrus.* (…) But tell me honestly, Socrates, do you believe this tale of mythology to be true?
>
> *Socrates.* Why, I should do nothing strangely out of the way if I *were* to refuse to it credit, as the learned do; and go on in their rationalizing method to say that as the girl was playing

> with Pharmacæa she was blown over the adjoining cliffs by a blast of wind Boreas; and that having met with her death in this manner, she was fabled to have been carried off by the god Boreas – either from this place, or if you like from Mars's hill (…) But for my part, Phædrus, though I consider such explanations sufficiently pretty, yet I esteem them the peculiar province of a very subtle, painstaking, and by no means particularly enviable person; if for no other reason than that he will be called upon, as soon as he has finished this subject, to set us right as to the form of the Hippocentaurs, and again as to that of the Chimæra, and then he will have pouring in upon him a like crowd of Gorgons and Pegasuses, and such a wondrous host of portentous and impossible creations, that if he were to disbelieve them all, and, with a kind of vulgar acuteness, apply to each successively the test of probability, he would require no small amount of time and labour to his task. But I have no leisure for such studies.
>
> (Plato 1927, 229c)

Socrates gives reason for not taking mythology to task, but in so doing he acknowledges that the learned spend their time in rationalizing method, demanding answers to questions that naturally arise from mythology. To be sure, scepticism predates modern philosophy.

In architecture, the ædicule is a home in which a god dwells. 'No it isn't!' science tells us. Yet there is a deeper idea that insists, 'The ædicule is a home in which a god dwells.' Imagine that.

We have seen that for Aristotle, Hume and Kant, imagination has a central role in the process of perception. Perception relies upon our ability to do two things (at least). It enables us to recognize this thing presented to me in my understanding as a dog; that is, a dog as opposed to a doormat or a dragon. It also enables us to recognize that *this* dog, now drinking water in the kitchen, is the same dog that was, a minute ago, chewing a bone in my study. In each of the two cases, something absent from immediate perception is required to shape that perception. All three agree that the faculty responsible for this process is imagination. Since Hume is hamstrung by his empiricist convictions, he is unable to regard imagination without suspicion. It is, for him, tantamount to a bad habit, but one he is addicted to because without it, there is no explanation available to him for the unity of self over time. Whilst imagination is central to his account, it remains a feature of his thinking to which he is bound to take a sceptical view.

For our purposes, we should now look at the role imagination plays in Kant's theory of perception. Kant supposes perception to be built out of sensibility, a passive capacity of the mind to register qualities, for instance colour and sound. To this he adds understanding. Now, he has established space and time as intuitions (i.e., as we have seen, they are not derived from sensibility but are necessary for there to be sensible qualities upon which to operate). The categories, those *a priori* concepts which were to provide the form of our thoughts about the world at the most abstract level, operate upon the qualities delivered by sensibility. It is the imagination that now enters the complex manifold of perception by imposing order upon the sensibly given, bringing them under empirical concepts, themselves applications of the most general *a priori* concepts.

Thus, imagination brings understanding to imprint itself upon sensibility and give form (ultimately governed by the categories) to the qualities arising from sensibility. In the manifold of perception, the understanding writes its conceptual content over that which sensibility provides. Imagination, that is, enables us to have perceptions that are about the world – they represent the world. We are able to look out into the world and to describe what we see (or hear or taste or smell or feel). We are able, at the same time, to say what the world is like.

The great achievement of the first critique is to have synthesized rationalist and empirical principles into a unified explanation of mind, the seat of thought. However, to 'say is' is not to 'see as', and this last is to be the subject of the next chapter.

5

Imagination unhinged

I Imagination let loose

What is the imagined intentional object of experience in architecture? We remember from our discussion of Sartre and his notion of kinds of consciousness, that he inherits the view of intentionality by which consciousness is directed upon an object. Thus, our question is: upon what aspect of architecture is our consciousness directed? Before answering that question, we need to look again at the nature of aesthetic experience and the nature of beauty in Kant's thought. We do so because Kant writes of the fine arts as communicating aesthetic ideas. Their place in his aesthetics is important for architecture, if it is to be demonstrated that it is a fine art.

Kant spends the first book of the *Critique of Judgement* dealing with judgements of beauty (Kant 1987). In the third of four moments comprising book I, he introduces the notion of 'adherent beauty'. Until then we have been considering pure beauty. Cases of pure beauty are as when we judge something beautiful independently of any concept being brought to bear. For instance, when I look at a section cut across a nautilus and regard its form, I make the judgement that it is beautiful. The thought of what it is (meant to be) does not enter into the judgement. (I might not know what it is at which I look, being in ignorance as to the submarine world to which it belongs; or bracketing such knowledge as I have, out of *this* experience.) My judgement is purely formal. I attend to the configuration of the complex visual object and its parts, and see in it a unity that exhibits purposiveness, yet whilst I see it independently of any *determinate* purpose that it (and its inter-related parts) makes manifest. It simply looks as if it is designed to some unspecified end.

We might otherwise wonder: 'What is it supposed to do?' 'How does it work?' 'What purpose does it serve?' However, judging it to be purely beautiful puts such questions aside.

The problem Kant has is to show that the felt pleasure we take in looking at the nautilus – precisely because it is a *felt* pleasure – yet has the force of judgement within it. That is to say, no concept is applied to the object of my pleasure and yet I regard the pleasure as grounding a 'judgement' that, being a judgement, is recommended to other similarly constituted observers. The judgement is, because there is no conceptual constraint upon the object of my pleasure, made solely and immediately in virtue of the particular kind of pleasure to which it gives rise. Given the structure Kant imposes upon perception, as we saw in the last chapter, it is appropriate to note that in such cases as the nautilus, he writes of 'the free play of imagination'.

FIGURE 5.1 *Nautilus Cuttaway.* © *Chris 73/Wikimedia Commons, 2004.*

I am able to put aside the otherwise pressing questions, 'What is it?', 'How am I to use it?' and those other questions mentioned above. In regarding the thing as beautiful, I am able to allow my imagination to think of it only as a formal presentation, allowing me to notice the way in which it is formally arranged, *as if to some purpose*, I know not what, nor care. That this is an experience freed from the cognitive necessities that ordinarily apply to perception, the experience is disconnected from its usual function; let loose.

Concepts are, *ex-hypothesi*, absent from the judgement of pure beauty, and the imagination is relieved of its mundane duty in cognition. What, then, is the role of imagination in its free play, and how does it help us to understand this liberated application as it is recruited to aesthetic judgement?

When I make a judgement of pure beauty, I am able to submit incoming sensations, 'intuitions', to the free play of my imagination, unfettered by the usual constraints obtaining in perception. This is the basis of Kant's formalism. In his argument for formal beauty – pure beauty – Kant makes an extraordinary claim. For *feelings* are essentially subjective. And so claiming it is a *judgement*, and that the scope of judgement is extended over all rational creatures, makes it look pretty odd. After all, we wouldn't want to say that my preference for chicken dhansak over chicken korma shows a lack of sensitivity or imagination; let alone that it might be the basis for our falling out. ('How dare you prefer dhansak?', 'How could you like korma?')

However, when my judgement is an expression of the pleasure that I take in the form of a nautilus, it has a dimension which calls upon the cognitive faculties in a way that the food preferences do not. For in the judgement of the beauty of the nautilus I attend to features of the complex presentation and see in their unity what Kant calls purposiveness. That is to say that I see the presentation as belonging to a world in which design can be discerned, even when I am fully aware there is no perceived purpose that its parts disclose; and even though, since Charles Darwin's *Origin of the Species*, I know that the shell at which I gaze was *not* designed. It is not *as* a nautilus that I judge the formal presentation as beautiful. The judgement of pure beauty says something substantial about us, and who we are. It tells us that, being so constituted as a community, we find (or we *should* find) pleasure in the *apparent* purposiveness of the formal configuration of a presentation.

II Beauty under the reign of concepts

Pure beauty is one thing; dependent beauty quite another. It is not until section 16 in book I that Kant then discusses 'adherent beauty'. There, he admits that sometimes we do call something beautiful after its classification as being an example of this or that kind of object – thus bringing the object under a regulative concept. There is little doubt that Kant thinks of adherent beauty as inferior to pure beauty, where nature provides the clearest examples. But even within nature we can think of examples of adherent beauty – as when we discuss the sheen of a dog's coat, the brightness of its eyes, its graceful movement as it chases a ball. Each of these descriptions applies to its beauty *as a dog*. (No boy, however beautiful, would look beautiful, *as a boy*, scampering on all fours, chasing a ball, and then panting and looking unquestioningly up at his mistress awaiting the next throw of the ball.) Pure beauty or 'free beauty' is the main focus of book I, with considered asides on the lower nature of adherent beauty.

III The importance of art for Kant: Its beauty considered

We must persevere with Kant until section 43 of book I for his discussion of art in general, before moving onto fine art in section 44. Interestingly, since Kant has had such influence over the fine arts, it might seem surprising at first that he considers the fine arts to be adherent beauties. Conceptual constraint hangs over the objects of fine art, marshalling each of them under a regulative concept – as a painting, as a poem, as a work of architecture. This division of beauty between pure and adherent presents difficulties for architecture, when considered as a fine art. However, it also presents an opportunity to get clear about the nature of architecture as a fine art that nevertheless has utility as an essential element (as was noted in part one of this book).

The arts are a special case of dependent beauty. It is *as an art* that I find works beautiful – notwithstanding the tendency in modernism to conflate found objects, especially those exhibiting a certain charm, with fine art. (Duchamp did not make this mistake. He was chasing after another prize.)

If architecture is to escape the burden of mechanically working out solutions to building tasks, it must un-yoke itself from the mantle of mere 'craft'. Only then can it really establish itself as a fine art. If it cannot, then it must settle itself down to work in the mechanical application of skills handed down and learnt by rote. Such skills are valuable: and, therefore, enviable and laudable; but they do not, either severally or in concert, amount to the manifest originality required by the fine artist in the fruition of her work. If architecture amounts to no more than the acquired habits of a particular set of skills, then it is a mechanical art. If it is a fine art, then more needs to be said about its aesthetic nature; and if it is to qualify as a fine art, we shall need to see what it is for its works to achieve such recognition and, therefore, how they are to be appreciated.

It is to Kant that we return for discrimination between mechanical and aesthetic arts:

> If art merely performs the acts that are required to make a possible object actual, adequately to our *cognition* of that object, then it is *mechanical* art; but if what it intends directly is [to arouse] the feeling of pleasure, then it is called *aesthetic* art. The latter is either *agreeable* or *fine* art. It is agreeable art if its purpose is that the pleasure should accompany presentations that are merely *sensations*; it is fine art if its purpose is that the pleasure should accompany presentations that are *ways of cognizing*.
>
> (Kant 1987, 172)

We should note that in this passage Kant specifically mentions that agreeable art and fine art each have a determinate purpose. (His scheme is set out in Figure 5.2.)

Mechanical art, therefore, is the art of making something according to how we normally conceive of the resultant object; such as, since the Industrial Revolution, a Lancashire clogger fashions a pair of clogs using a hard wood for the sole, for instance, alder – the wood reinforced with strips of steel in the manner of a horse-shoe; or a Bordeaux vintner, whose vinification integrates the flavour of wood from the barrel with the grape in the production of claret; or the Parisian mixologist who puts together her claridge,

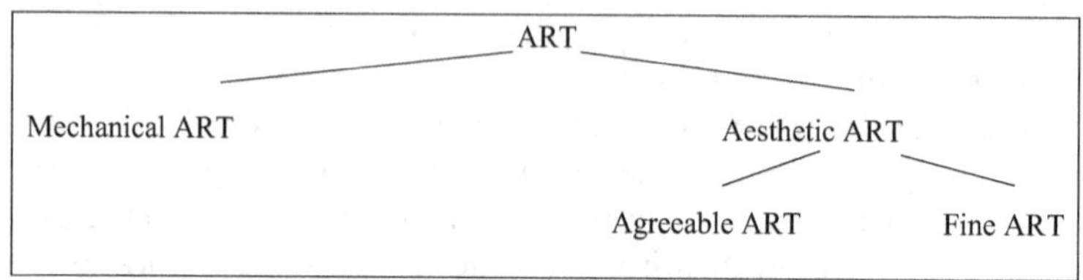

FIGURE 5.2 *Kant's divisions of art.*

an apricot cocktail, perhaps as served in the Bec-de-Gaz bar in Montparnasse. For clogs, clarets and claridges are not works of fine art. They are the products of local crafts bequeathed from generation to generation. The apprentice learns through imitation and repetition such skills as are required to sustain the practice. 'What is she doing?' 'She's making clogs/ fermenting claret/ fixing us a claridge.' The result is a work of mechanical art. Tomorrow she will follow the same procedure; and the next day will unfold accordingly, and so on through the generations. We do not delight in the *originality* of the clogs or the claret or the claridge. Rather, we delight in their constancy and consistency of form. We become hefted to these objects as their makers became hefted to the practice of making them.

Aesthetic art, by contrast, is *essentially*, a source of pleasure in the object itself. In his consideration of aesthetic art, Kant distinguishes between *agreeable* and *fine* arts. The former is typified by the pleasure we take in the dinner party conversation. Its purpose is 'mere enjoyment'. Conversations are not prescribed. The lively, witty and charming participants in a conversation enjoy the event as entertainment. It has no purpose other than such pleasure.

The appreciation of fine art, by contrast, is a particular kind of pleasure. Over and above the pleasure we might take in mere sensations, we take pleasure in engaging the intellect with the presentations of fine art. Kant, having written that fine art has, 'as its purpose (…) that the pleasure should accompany presentations that are *ways of cognizing*' writes the page following, 'Fine art (…) is a way of presenting that is purposive on its own and that furthers, even though without purpose, the culture of our mental powers to [facilitate] social communication' (Kant 1987, 306).

The special place Kant affords fine art within adherent beauty shows his regard for works of art and his conferment of great status on those who practise within the various media. Moreover, according to Kant, it is within these media we are able to discern a special kind of value. For fine art proffers the hope of achieving the status of genius, an eminence, as we have already noted, beyond the grasp of scientists and other brilliant men and women of distinction. We turn, now, to a number of technicalities pertaining to our understanding of fine art as the art of genius.

Common to all judgements of beauty is the range of their claim. This is sometimes referred to as the antinomy of taste. We have come across this already when differentiating between the judgements of beauty and expressions of mere preference. The antinomy runs like this: if the judgement of beauty is connected with pleasure then it is subjective. If, however, it is a *judgement*, then it calls upon the agreement of others. In the Indian restaurant example, there is no dispute between she, who would prefer chicken korma, and I, who would prefer chicken dhansak.

However, in fine art, as elsewhere in our appreciation of beauty, the judgement calls upon reason. I have a strong feeling that anyone who thought Picasso's *Guernica* childish, or Miles Davies' *Sketches of Spain* untuneful, or Mies' German pavilion clumsy, would have missed the point; and I would note their *judgement* is in dispute with mine; and that the disputants should seek to resolve their differences. *Perhaps*, it is I who have missed the point – being eager to appear modern. Alternatively, I could be charged with judging too safely. I have judged too conservatively, choosing early modern; and so I champion Picasso's painting and Miles Davis's music, whilst she, more adventurously, judges Picasso too clumsy in his depiction of women in their raw distress; as if they were unable to cope with the horror of war. She thinks Miles Davis too undisciplined in the manner of his use of Spanish folk melody and in his re-interpretation of Manuel de Falla's *El Concierto de Aranjuez*. She points me towards Osvaldo Golijov. His *Pasión según de San Marcos*, she judges, more ably appropriates folk music into jazz/classical; and she thinks Mies too stade, to constricted, when compared to the liveliness of Gehry's Guggenheim Museum in Bilbao. Nevertheless, it certainly looks as if there is a conversation to be had; reasons to be put forward and inspected, weighed up, secured or put aside, which is simply not the case in the Indian restaurant.

How, then, are we to account for beauty as it is to be found within the various media of the fine arts? In Chapter 3, we looked at Lopes' 'buck passing' theory and noted its advantages over the institutional theory in dealing with the 'hard cases'. Since the hard cases were designed by artists to resist the constraints of theory, and the institutional theory was designed by theorists to accommodate the hard cases, it is illuminating that Lopes' alternative offers both a more liberal and a more constrictive view of how the arts are best dealt with. It is liberal in the space that it opens up for the discussion between philosophers, critics, art historians, artists and other interested parties to bring into focus their varied and overlapping perspectives. It is constrictive in that it secures a place for the history of the medium previously thought to have been dispensed with by the hard cases and sustained by the institutional theory.

IV The role of the free play of imagination in fine art

To 'Say is' is not to 'see as', was the slightly obscure end of our last chapter. That is because describing something says something about it that is either true or false. If I see a dog in the field outside and say so, I make a description of how the world is. If, however, I *see* a paint smeared canvas *as* a man's face, then I am not *saying* anything *is*. 'Saying is' describes the world; 'seeing as' is a state of mind that entertains descriptions that are not claimed to be true. In his *Art and Imagination* (1974), Scruton argues there are two intentional objects in this second case. There is the intentional object of my seeing the flat, coloured, painted canvas – the material object of my experience; and there is the other intentional object, the face, that is imagined. But this imagined face inheres in the paint marks. So, the imaginative object of experience is co-instantiated with the seen object of perceptual experience. As Wollheim has it, the face is 'seen in' the paint marks. Importantly, both intentional objects are experienced simultaneously.

Scruton goes on to think of the aesthetic experience of all the fine arts as manifesting double intentionality (Scruton 2012). We hear the movement in the music, for instance. We hear a succession of sounds – the material intentional object; and we hear them as moving in relation to one another. We simultaneously hear movement *in* the sounds we perceive. However, the 'movement' is as imaginary as the face we see in the coloured marks across the surface of the canvas. For nothing actually moves when we 'hear' the movement in the sounds.

Whilst it is wise to caution against mechanical images of cognition, it is ever tempting to think of the various faculties of perception – sensibility and understanding – as being synthesized by yet another: imagination. Whilst both Aristotle and Hume regarded imagination as an addition to the complex list of ingredients required for cognition, Kant regards imagination as transcendent. It is what must be presupposed in order for there to be perception, and hence knowledge, of any description.

In the free play of imagination, however, we seek neither direct perception nor direct knowledge. So, Kant thinks of the role of imagination – in both the making and the apprehension of fine art – as disengaged: or, so to speak: freewheeling.

In so thinking, conceptualization remains a constituent faculty of thought. It is simply ungoverned by the effort to achieve that particular contact with the world required for our participation in the quotidian tasks of human commerce. Unhinged from its workaday duty in perception, the imagination seeks epiphany; and, in its two stages, it finds its home in fine art.

Here, the simplest of phenomena prove fertile for the exercise of the imagination, as when we look to the clouds (*de re*), momentarily putting aside the concept (*de dicto*) and putting in its place another, say 'a great sea battle', or 'the fierce faces of the angry gods looking down upon us'. We try on these conceptually constrained mantles, aligning their contours to the presentation provided by the clouds, amusing ourselves between the points of contact and the discrepancies that obtain between them. It is, as it were, an entertainment of non-veridical conceptual content, supervening upon veridical perception.

Beyond this freedom lies a second. For there are epiphanic experiences to be shaped and to be undertaken which lie beyond our conceptual grasp. And *these* experiences rest upon the deliberate *misconceptions* established by the first set of imaginative freedoms.

It is here that Kant writes of *aesthetic ideas*. As noted earlier, he gives the example of poetry – for Kant this fine art proudly sits upon the throne of all the arts. Using words (and through them their designated concepts) the poet yet fashions in language the idea of that which lies *beyond* concepts.

> [B]y aesthetic idea I mean a presentation of the imagination which prompts much thought, but to which no determinate thought whatsoever, i.e., no [determinate] *concept*, can be adequate, so that no language can express it completely and allow us to grasp it. It is easy to see that an aesthetic idea is the counterpart (pendant) of a *rational idea*, which is, conversely, a concept to which no *intuition* (presentation of the imagination) can be adequate.
>
> (Kant 1987, 314)

The examples he gives of the poet's aesthetic ideas are those of death, love and envy, amongst others (idem.). It is a mark of the fine arts that they afford us, through imagination, the ability to grasp such aesthetic ideas through experience; as opposed to rational ideas which are understood through abstract concepts to which no sensation can be adequate.

Such experiences secured through fine art are, *ex hypothesi*, beyond the scope of conceptual analysis. On that account, they are presentations of the epiphanic. Through these experiences, we come to a 'symbolic' view of the world unavailable to mere description. It is here we might remember Jung in Africa *feeling* the need to find a 'mythology of our own', whilst attempting to express his feeling of *déjà vu*.

Whilst Kant rightly goes for the magnificence of love and death, for instance, it is worth pointing out that epiphanies can also be experienced in the presence of small miracles: as when Seamus Heaney writes of his first Conway Stewart fountain pen. His description of the sound of the pen snorkling up its first fill of ink as the shopkeeper demonstrates the pen's mechanism takes us into the moment and its intensity. The intensity presents to us the slow passing of time as the narrator's loneliness is anticipated (of his going away to school). The loneliness is revealed to us (but never described) (Heaney 2018, 156). It is not something we read off from the text. Rather it is the seat of a deep feeling that defies description. To understand the poem is not to have some new knowledge. It is to *feel* something and to recognize in that experience, its profundity.

Now, following Lopes' argument that each fine art must be practised within medium-specific parameters, we should augment his buck passing theory with a requisition for examples of aesthetic ideas shown forth by each of the fine arts. Following Lopes' interdisciplinary ambitions, it is to the art historians and critics to whom we should turn for the most illustrative models.

Before doing that for architecture, however, we need to consider what an aesthetic idea could look like in this field. Where, we must ask ourselves, must we direct our attention in search of architectural epiphanies?

6

Architecture: Beauty in service

I Women weavers of Navajo narratives

In her book, *Worn*, a study of the history of clothes, Sofi Thanhauser describes meeting Velma, a contemporary Navajo weaver in Mesa, a border town outside Phoenix. (Thanhauser 2022). Velma explains the modern history of Navajo weaving as an intertwining of the rugs' creation, to be worn by her people. She speaks of the narration of personal and community histories contemplated during the fabrication of those rugs. The textile designs play a role in the generation of conversations concerning the history of family members and tribal matters – rather in the way that a family might gather round a photograph album to recall the incidents of family and community, and to provide personal and familiar histories to those interested: the young, the old, the family, the tribe. She goes on to write of the influence of the Navajo rug on American modernists in fine art, and documents the exhibitions that sought to connect them, including *Color Riot*, at the Heard Museum in Phoenix, 2019. The show was initially developed as a way of juxtaposing the work of the Navajos with that of the German émigré, Josef Albers, former professor at Bauhaus, Dessau. It subsequently grew to fill the entire exhibition area.

The exhibition contained works by Navajo women during the 'transitional period', in the 1860s. This short-lived period, during which the Navajo were interned at Bosque Redondo, New Mexico, saw intertribal trading and brought the Navajo weavers into contact with the brightly coloured poncho designs of the Santillo weavers of northern Mexico. This trading had brought dyed cottons from Mexico through the pueblos of New Mexico.

It was in the pueblos that we first met Ochwiay Biano, Jung's interlocutor. Thus, we return to wonder about art, design and the nature of storytelling in a culture whose mythological accounts are motivated by a coherence of the social group in a world that is not in a position to consider the scientific alternative. The textile art of the Navajos is designed to make sense of their social attachments. Thanhauser, writing of the discrepancy between the idea of art as mythological storytelling, and the rarefied conception of a more sophisticated high art, champions the former as more authentic. She regards it as beautiful in its establishment of social connections and family bonds. Whereas the sophisticated high art is deemed beautiful just because it is set free from any social or utilitarian urgency. By way of bringing this into focus and, in so doing, ridiculing the separation of aesthetics from life, Thanhauser remarks,

> Albers' wife, the textile artist Anni Albers, headed a weaving workshop at the Bauhaus, one of the few women to hold a senior role at the school. Anni Albers described weaving this way: 'Like any craft it may end in producing useful objects, or it may rise to the level of art.' She implies that 'useful objects' fell below 'art' on a hierarchy of importance. For the Navajo, however, weavings were to become 'art' when the violent intervention of the U.S. government robbed the Navajo of subsistence, and they were forced to cater to western taste by producing weavings that had no other purpose than to hang on a wall.
>
> (Thanhauser 2022, 276)

This discrepancy was, of course, something the exhibition was meant to point up and deny. The attitude adopted was that the Navajo women's work could be seen as coextensive with what Josef Albers was doing in his paintings. The Bauhaus could be seen in its modernist approach as regarding the engagement between visual arts disciplines as firmly set upon an equal footing. (Although trained as a painter, Albers went on to teach design at Yale.) Nevertheless, fine art could also be seen as the purest. Thus, whatever the intentions of the curation of 'Color Riot', Albers' paintings could also be interpreted as a distillation of what the Navajo women were unknowingly doing; a fine art 'purification' of the everyday enjoyment of colour design by 'naïve' artists. Thanhauser adds that beneath the tapestries of the Navajo women, '[t]he wall tags beneath each work read, "Unidentified artist"'.

There is no doubt Thanhauser has in mind the consideration of Navajo rugs as works of art neglected by Western aesthetics. (We have already seen that the ancients had no similar conception of fine art, regarding mimesis as a feature of some, but by no means all, practices of making; for which they had the term 'techne', translated, depending on the context, as 'art' or more usually, 'skill'.) A little later in her book, describing an exhibition, 'Indian Art of the United States' at MoMA in New York in 1941, Thanhauser adds,

> Although the 1941 show (...) was correct to assert that Navajo images were every bit as full of genius as other types of modern art, it imposed a western conception of art – a conception that had been, since the industrial revolution, willing to strip creativity from the making of everyday objects like clothes and furniture and corral that creativity all within one small ghetto: the making of useless objects known as 'art.'
>
> (Thanhauser 2022, 277–8)

Denied their intended role of being rugs within which the tribes told stories, both personal and communal, and their purpose of being rugs and blankets to be worn, the Navajo tapestries became those 'useless' things to hang on walls. The Navajo women, without any such artistic intention, had achieved the status of 'fine artists', in the post-enlightenment conception of those practices. However, that achievement came at the cost of what it was their tradition might otherwise have bequeathed. That view doesn't hold water. Something has to give.

Either we treat the rugs and blankets as crafts – beautifying arts – or we have to redraw the conception of fine art from which they would have to be excluded. Certainly, the Navajo women were making the rugs and blankets *intentionally*. And the intention was to make objects that could be used for both warmth and decoration. They were clearly made within, and as part of, a culture. The storytelling together with the communal conversations secures this much. However, unless we can cross the bridge between utility and beauty, it looks as if, according to the women's intentions, the Navajo women are beautifying artists and their work is not fine art.

One solution to the problem is to think of the modernists as having climbed down from the pedestal of fine art and to have seen their work as visual art, continuous with design more generally. That move can surely be traced in the coming together of various visual arts disciplines in the art schools. It is the basis upon which Bauhaus was established. Recall that this is the basis upon which Meyer re-named the 'Department of Architectue' as the 'Department of Building'.

However, another solution, suggested to us by the systematization of the visual arts and augmented by the philosophical approach adopted by Lopes, is to regard the tapestries as belonging to a fine art-kind *different* from the painting of Josef Albers. We could, thereby, keep the distinction between fine art-kinds and other crafts, whilst acknowledging that works of fine art are adherent beauties. Kant is again a resource.

Thanhauser's book is a celebration of the clothes of people. Its interest stretches beyond that remit – into furniture, as the last quote suggests. Here is Kant on the works of cabinet makers. In defining architecture he writes that, along with sculpture, it belongs to plastic art. He goes on,

> [T]emples, magnificent buildings for public gatherings, or again residences, triumphal arches, columns, cenotaphs, and so on, erected as honorary memorials, belong to architecture; we may even add to this all household furnishings (such as the work of the cabinet maker and other such things that are meant to be used). For what is essential in a *work of architecture* is the product's adequacy for a certain use.
>
> (Kant 1987, 323)

We might, then, take from Kant's licence, that the Navajo women were practising fine artists working within the art-kind: architecture. Unlike a shoemaker, a vintner and a cocktail mixer, the Navajo women set to work each day on unique pieces that were not simply repetitions of previous works. Their days are not so mechanistically circumscribed. With this extension of what we should include in the fine art of architecture, we turn again to look at how our idea of dwelling impinges upon our conception of architecture.

II Gottfried Semper's four elements

The strategy taken in the development of this book is to look to thinkers from within and beyond architecture for their variously informed wisdom. Whilst Semper was a distinguished architect, theorist and educator, not all of what he has to say fits the trajectory upon which we travel. Yet, some of his insights call upon us to revise our conception of the ancients and the classicism that seeks its authority from them. It is, perhaps, an irony that in reaching beyond antiquity, we find an argument that supports some form of modernism.

In his *The Four Elements of Architecture*, first published in 1851, Semper identifies four elements (Semper 1989). These are: (i) *the hearth*, which is at the centre of the idea of building and is its *moral* core. Framing the hearth are the remaining three elements; (ii) *the roof* above provides a shelter for the hearth and altar and, of course, protects the flame from rain, hail, sleet and snow; (iii) *the enclosure* surrounding separates the private from the public realms and shields the flame from wind; and (iv) *the mound* beneath provides a pedestal for the hearth. Around the hearth the meal is prepared and the body revived after the hunt. Here is to be found the first social gatherings. It is the enclosure that takes us to the idea of weaving once more:

> But what primitive technique evolved from the *enclosure*? None other than the *wall fitter* (...), that is, the weaver of mats and carpets. This statement may appear strange and requires an explanation.
>
> (...) [T]here are writers who devote much time to searching for the origin of art and who believe they can deduce from it all the different ways of building. The nomadic tent plays rather an important role in their arguments. Yet while with great acumen they detect in the catenary curve of the tent the norm of the Tartar-Chinese way of building (although the same shapes occur in the caps and shoes of these people), they overlook the more general and less dubious influence that the carpet in its capacity as a *wall*, as a vertical means of protection, had on the evolution of certain architectural forms. Thus I seem to stand without the

> support of a single authority when I assert that the carpet wall plays a most important role in the general history of art.
>
> (Semper 1989, 103)

Semper's architectural work is eclectic but otherwise unremarkable, and does not ring with the chimes of his broader thinking. That does not prevent us from using his theoretical writing as a means of developing a theory of architecture to which he would not subscribe. He might have claimed reason alone gave him authority to give such importance to the carpet wall. After all, we started off in Chapter 1 by considering what might have brought architecture into being as a concern for human culture. The classicists refer us to the primitive hut in their speculative pondering upon *Ur-architecture*. That is no more (and no less) than a mythological account. Why shouldn't Semper help himself to an explanation, especially if that has more persuasive clout?

Harry Francis Mallgrave, architect, theorist, university professor and historian, in his introduction to Semper's *Four Elements*, remarks upon the intellectual climate at the time. He notes, for instance, that in the eighteenth and nineteenth centuries, both science and art subscribed to the Creation myth as the basis of their study of mankind. That account, authorized by the Bible, put the creation of the world at 4004 BC; and so, Semper's writing reached beyond such historical accounts with his adherence to the newer theories in which the world, and humanity in it, had existed for millenia.

During these pre-classical years, according to Semper, there is evidence of enclosures for keeping animals made from woven fencing. The four elements are really identified through human motive, rather than their being bits or units that, assembled together, produce architecture. After having set out the elements, he sets out to explain their history. That of enclosure has prominence. As Mallgrave writes in his introduction to Semper's book,

> [He] focuses on the 'enclosure' and begins to outline what later becomes central to his thinking: the metamorphosis of the motive into the idea of 'dressing' (Bekleidung). He [rejects the] mimetic basis for architectural form in favor of a thematic

> one: the braided or woven wall mats hung vertically and invented before clothing according to some ethnographic accounts. The motive, Semper reasons, first emerged in the crude intertwining of tree branches for fences and pens (chronicled for existing aboriginal tribes), evolved into the art of weaving with bast and wicker, later with woven threads. The perfection of the textile phase of this motive took place in ancient Assyria and Persia, cultures that were famed for their colorful tents and tapestries.
>
> (Mallgrave 1989, 24)

The mention of tents and tapestries serves to sever the ties with mimetic claims of the classicists. In his acknowledgement of an architectural history predating Greco-Roman antiquity, Semper removes the archetypal status of the primitive hut; we are no longer under the power of its authority.

The removal of one mythical origin of architecture reconfigures our search for others. Semper isn't looking for a single unified account of how architecture emerged from dwelling. His 'four elements' are somehow misnamed. For they are, in Semper's account, not *bits* of architectural detail to be assembled as might a children's building set. Rather, the elements are to be seen as our responses to pre-dispositional needs. They are, in Semper's word, responses to our 'motives'. No single building is identified as *the* origin of architecture. Provided with the four motives, we are enabled to search for various solutions depending on our mode of living. So, 'tents and tapestries' are suitable solutions for nomadic peoples. They provide suitable response to a more general motive, shared with our own architecture, but tailored to the need of a wandering populous.

Looking back beyond the classical period allows Semper to posit different cultural responses to these general motives. A-historically, however, it licenses our perception of modernism as a valid response to the motives, once the grip of mimesis has been loosened. Semper's motives become archetypes. We are pre-disposed, motivated, to build in response to these urgencies.

Both Thanhauser's Navajo weavers and Semper's aboriginal fence-makers have, in the accounts we are given, a sense of community that is the basis for the art or prototypical art in which the practitioners are immersed. Oddly, it is 'the hanging on a wall', as useless art, that so aggrieves Thanhauser. It is 'the hanging on the wall' as coloured enclosure, that Semper celebrates as the root of architecture as an art. Here we must find in each account the grounds of reconciliation. That reconciliation is to be found in the art-kind, architecture.

III Kant and Wont

It is time to recall Kant's *sensus communis*. In Part One, we saw that Kant was dissatisfied with the idea of common sense being an argument sufficient to trump good reason. However, that was a means of clarifying the *sensus communis* he uses, himself, to shore up the nature of aesthetics when it comes to the universality of judgement. To whom does the *sensus communis* belong?

It has been the subtext, thus far, that *we*, who are rational persons, comprise the *sensus communis*. It belongs to us in the same way that our bodies belong to us. We *are* the *sensus communis*. We are a gathering of bodies assembled into one collective body. When identified with that body, *it* acts as it is *wont*. Within that body we need not agree; but in our disagreements, *we are able to*, whether we do or not, come to a rational agreement on matters of mathematics (whether, for instance, there could be a greatest prime number), optimum medical procedures, cost-benefit analysis of said procedures; efficient means of travelling by public transport; the reliability of the weather forecast; the best procedures for lowering carbon emissions; the suitable punishments for the theft of a pensioner's life-savings (with adjustments for mitigating circumstances); and we can decide whether or not Stonborough House (the Wittgenstein House) in the modernist style on the Kundmanngasse, Vienna, is to count as a work of fine art. We can also agree upon a procedure for thinking about how best to consider the worth of Wittgenstein's building, if and when we decide it is a work of art. That is not to say that we shall agree, but only that it lies within our rational agency to do so. This, I feel sure, is what Kant meant by the *sensus communis*. It is subject to, and not opposed to, reason.

IV Wont as the consciousness directed to service

Earlier in our conversation we dwelt upon dwelling, and it was in those preliminary ruminations that we considered Jung's perusals concerning archetypes. Jung sought to establish a collective unconscious in which we share narrative accounts of our world. It is, as it were, an innate tendency we have to posit agency more powerful than any human capacity, which accounts for events in the world to which we are subjected. So, for instance, there is a human tendency to conceive of deity as all providential. Hence, it is *reasonable* for us to live a prayerful life; and this, we find across cultures and peoples. We are pre-disposed to turn to such abstract accounts of the machinations of the weather, of ill health, of natural disasters and of death. All of which are, more or less, mysteries.

The English word 'wont' comes to us from the German, via Old English '*wonan*', meaning 'to dwell' or 'be accustomed to'. We saw that our understanding of architecture was bound up with the pre-disposition to dwell, and that if architecture is a fine art it must be accreted upon the primitive nature of our finding shelter. However, such accretion departs from the primitive in becoming fine art.

A question now to be faced is this: What is the relationship between the 'collective unconscious', 'pre-disposition', 'archetype' and fine art generally, and architecture in particular? Herein, we must call upon our grasp of the nature of the history of fine art and its contribution to, and constraint upon, the making of new art. If the instinct to build is primitive, how then does this rudimentary ground secure the cultivated status for the architecture it underwrites as a fine art?

Relying upon our notion of the special adherent beauty of fine art developed by Kant, we can develop an account of the *medium* of architecture. It will be helpful, as ever, to argue from analogy. In Wollheim's analysis of depiction – a preliminary to his analysis of painting – he helps himself to the notion of pareidolia. This phenomenon is, he tells us, a natural capacity we have perchance. It is a brute fact that we can see representational content in patterns – what Wollheim calls 'representational seeing'.

It is the capacity to see visual content (for instance a face) in the patterns of, say, clouds; or in the embers of a fire. Just as our primitive ability to see faces in clouds or in fires funds the fine art of painting, so too does our collective search for settlement, shelter and community fund the fine art of architecture. Out of nature emerges fine art. That is compatible with the thought, expressed earlier, that fine art is not reducible to nature.

But to exercise the capacity of 'representational seeing', as Alberti advised his students to do – is not yet to engage in painting. In order to develop the medium of painting, it is necessary for its practitioners to make marks in such a way that they form patterns in which certain contents are to be readily seen. It is painting only when these pictures are made for aesthetic reasons.

PART THREE

The medium of architecture

7

The medium of architecture: From philosophy to criticism

I Buildings and works of architecture

If representational painting is a fine art, dependent upon, but not reducible to, the practice of depiction, we should seek an analogy within the fine art of architecture. We must show that architecture is dependent upon, but not reducible to, the practice of building.

However, the problem re-surfaces just in case we think of fine art as essentially non-utilitarian. (When Vitruvius listed *utilitas*, he was not thinking of architecture as a fine art.) For building has, as its *raison d'être*, utility.

The idea of art for art's sake, which in itself contains the idea of a useless object with 'no other purpose than to hang on a wall', can be seen as a misconception of the Romantics' reading of Kant. His doctrine of pure beauty which exhibited purposiveness *yet with no determinate purpose* warranted, under misconception, that pure beauty is simply a matter of judging some work beautiful in terms of its form alone. However, we have seen that Kant thought the fine arts *adherent beauties*, and so conceptual constraints apply. The concept of what the thing is supposed to be weighs upon our judgement. Moreover, the constraint upon each of the arts is for it to communicate aesthetic ideas. Architecture is not alone in having its purpose definitively written into its conception *as an art*.

Kant has this to say, specifically about architecture:

> *Architecture* is the art of exhibiting concepts of things that are possible *only through art*, things whose form does not have

> nature as its determining basis but instead has a chosen purpose, and of doing so in order to carry out that aim and yet also with aesthetic purposiveness. In architecture the main concern is what *use* is to be made of the artistic object, and this use is a condition to which the aesthetic ideas are confined.
>
> (Kant 1987, 322)

This neatly contrasts nature with function. For arts that do have nature as their determining basis, for instance painting and sculpture, the form is determined by nature. For architecture the form is determined not by nature but by purpose. However, the purpose determines architectural form by exhibiting concepts of things that are possible *only through art*.

We return, as promised, to Pritchard's *Ironbridge*. The beauty of this work of art is given by its purpose, *as a bridge*. That it is engineered is not in doubt. It is a work of art because it is meant to be seen and judged beautiful. It is not merely a feat of engineering. In regarding it as a work of architecture, we see the new material, cast iron, as permitting the span to appear lighter than stone bridges. We see the lines that form the arches *as if* drawn, so that, as in Aristotle's observation on outline drawing, we see the resistance to forces that bear down upon the bridge. It becomes, as it were, a diagram of forces in action.

II The medium

There is much outwith the corpus of architecture attempting to push our view either hither or thither. Beyond aesthetics, political polemic bombards us from all sides. To make things more complicated, the ethical and the political are sometimes, at least, part of what makes a work of art beautiful. Content matters. However, if we leave the external ethical and political urgencies aside, where is the critical discourse within architecture that can enlighten us to the nature of its *medium*? For, whatever content a work of art delivers, it is of the medium in which the content is delivered that we seek illumination. Lyric writers, for instance, make works with widely different types of content. Bob Dylan writes both protest songs (e.g. 'The Times They Are a Changing') and love songs (e.g. 'Lay Lady Lay'). Yet, the medium of lyric writing remains removed from the content, even as the content contributes to the aesthetic experience of each work.

The British architect and theorist, Colin St John Wilson has written on Eliot's essay on tradition and the individual artist (St John Wilson 1992). He also calls upon that essay when writing on Erik Gunnar Asplund's move from classicism to modernism. In the former, St John Wilson more or less transposes Eliot's essay adapting it to architecture without any mention of a specific architectural genre. Like Eliot, he keeps within the confines of a discussion concerning *his* particular art, at its broadest, to the tradition from which it arises. He faces the problem of being 'new' or 'contemporary' whilst in some way responding to an entire history made present in the new architecture.

However, in the latter, he refers to Eliot in his discussion of Asplund's project for the Stockholm Chancellery. Asplund won the competition to build, with a set of neo-classical drawings in 1913. The project went through numerous changes and was eventually built in 1937 as a piece of modernism in the 'International Style'. Over the quarter century between the competition drawings and the finished building Asplund produced six alternative schemes – several neo-classical versions and the final modernist work. On the connection between classicism and modernism St John Wilson leans on Eliot,

> In Eliot's famous essay 'Tradition and the Individual Talent' he propounds a dynamic view of tradition as 'an easy commerce between the old and the new', which operates both ways, so that the new is modified by the past and the past, seen anew, by the introduction of the new. He emphasized the point that the really new meant an extension of the language to embrace an extension of sensibility, of awareness, of experience (…)
>
> There are things that [the classical language of architecture] cannot say and there are things so entrenched within it that it cannot shed them.
>
> (St John Wilson 1992, 142)

On the next page he quotes Herbert Read who had commented, 'In the back of every dictator can be found a bloody Doric column.'

In his polemical essay on Albert Speer, he loosens both barrells on Adolf Hitler's architect. Focusing on the New Chancellery in Berlin, he titles one section 'Long march to the scaffold', after the film of that name. The long march in question is a wonderful argument against *this* building in which St John Wilson takes a swipe at classicism. It's good criticism. However, it does not demolish classicism, even if it does, in the instance he sites, flatten both architect and client alike. 'The long march' is along corridors – circulation takes up 85 per cent of Speer's building. More tellingly, he compares Speer's use of *poche* space in his chancellery with that used in the 1922 competition entry by Asplund for the chancellery in Stockholm, one of the classicist versions. Speer cannot handle the odd geometry forced upon him by the site, whereas Asplund deals eloquently with similarly constrained spaces in his design. The floor plans of each provide the evidence for St John Wilson's argument.

> With Asplund two geometries are allowed an active presence, and the space between is activated by that dialectic to become a positive third term. For Speer *poche* is a way of obscuring the relationship between two geometries: it is merely a kind of inert

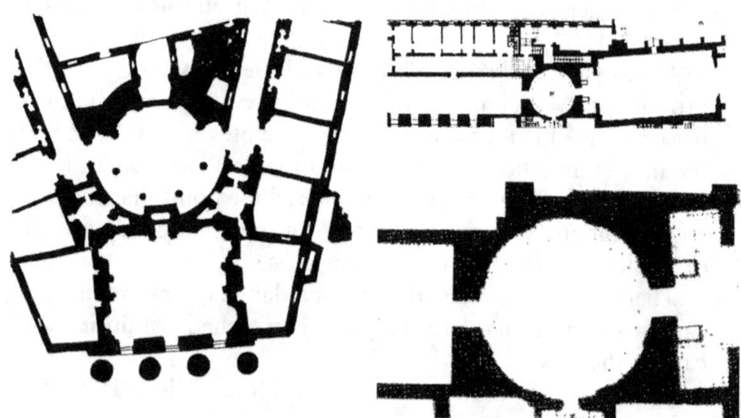

FIGURE 7.1 *Vanessa Perry, Comparison of Erik Gunnar Asplund,* Stockholm Chancelry *(left), and Albert Speer,* Berlin Chancelry *(right), 2022, (after Colin St John Wilson). Courtesy of the artist.*

> magma that allows him manically to straighten up bits that keep skidding out of his control.
>
> (St John Wilson 1992, 187)

Once, when visiting Rome on a study tour with the classicist Demitri Porphyrios and the students, we went to see Borromini's *San Carlo Alle Quattro Fontane*. In the cloister Demitri stretched out his arm, his palm upturned against the internal corner detail – the architrave between the ground and first floor – and remarked, 'Look at the architrave. It is fashioned out of chewing gum.' Seeing his point, I learned something about how a classicist might be appalled by baroque invention. 'Inert magma' and 'chewing gum' are not the stuff upon which the image of classical architecture draws its importance. The primitive builder, erecting his hut, had access to neither magma nor chewing gum. Porphyrios' aesthetic commitment to classicism persuaded him against the baroque detail. It disables him from *seeing* its beauty.

FIGURE 7.2 *Borromini, San Carlo alle Quattre Fontane, (Cloister), c.1638. © Chris Nas, 2007.*

St John Wilson continues,

The primary purpose of [Speer's building] is of course to glorify an upstart. We must ask what are the mechanisms employed to this end? Geoffrey Scott's gloss upon the theory of empathy provides some clue:

> The concrete spectacle ... has stirred our physical memory. It has awakened in us, not indeed an actual state of instability or of being overloaded, but that condition of spirit which in the past has belonged to our actual experiences of weakness, of thwarted effort or incipient collapse. We have looked at the building and identified ourselves with its apparent state. We have transcribed ourselves into terms of architecture.
>
> (St John Wilson 1992, 187–8)

Scott's quotation, from his *The Architecture of Humanism* (1914), is a reminder of the idea that we project properties onto our environment, and that, in this projection we fit ourselves into, or spread ourselves onto, the world.

III Architecture as an art

To be a fine artist, it is necessary to immerse oneself in the techniques developed through the history of the fine art which the practitioner has chosen. Immersion will be something along the lines of Kant's second nature. In the terms we have been discussing, this will mean that the artist will be able to manipulate her medium in such a way that the intentionality available through that medium engages the imagination of the spectator. This, in turn, puts an obligation on the artist, such that she, during the making of the work, must occupy the position of the spectator. She must, as it were, see the work from the spectator's point of view. This overall requirement accords with the view that the imagination is unhinged in its engagement with the work of art. It places the burden on both artist and spectator to recognize the imaginative object of intention in the object of perception. The ability to master the medium in this manner qualifies the artist in her chosen art-kind.

It is no accident that in the teaching of each of the arts, established practitioners take on the role of spectator in the criticism of student projects. The practitioners, as it were, persuade the student to see it from their more experienced point of view. In so doing, they can offer advice on how to improve the project within the terms of the criticism. So, tutors in architecture do not instruct. They suggest, they show – by pointing out the successful parts and pointing out the flaws. They guide the student in what is ultimately the student's responsibility for the design. This is true, also, of the other fine arts. Education is attained through suggestion within the context provided by each medium profile.

In the exchange that Alberti identifies, between the image of the building in mind and the process of drawing the building on paper; and between the drawing and the model, there is constant adjustment. These various realizations, up to and including the building's being constructed, traffic between the imagination and the medium. Such adjustment is in the nature of making any work in an art-kind. The clear idea is drawn out and then imprecision in the design comes to light. The adjusted drawing is made into a model, which in turn needs adjustment. There is a constant 'to-ing' and 'fro-ing' between the conception of the work and its various visual manifestations. *The architect learns about the building by looking at her drawing*. She learns how the drawing needs to be corrected by looking at the model she makes from the drawing. To better understand architecture we must learn to grasp its works through the translation back from building to plan, section and elevation – come to see three-dimensionally via our grasp of the two-dimensional representations. Just as we can learn to hear music by studying the structure of the score. In both musical and architectural cases, what we learn is to experience the work in a certain way. The score and the drawings are aids to that experience, but the experience to which each contributes is of the piece of music, in the one case, and of the building, in the other.

Further to mastering her medium, the artist, to be a great artist, must strive to make work that is original, in that it follows no prescribed rule from within the body of the history of the art-kind. Such an achievement is rare. Exhibition of genius in any specific art-kind is rare. Nevertheless, for there to be an art-kind, there must be practitioners. Not all of them can achieve the status as a genius. Kant tells us that there are methods and techniques that an artist must master in order to practise her art. However, these skills and techniques mastered, she must still strive for originality. That cannot come at once. First, she must immerse herself in the tradition. This will require acquaintance with the history of the art-kind in which she practises.

There are many practitioners who will be captivated by what is new and fresh and exhibits genius. They will gravitate towards these new developments but without necessarily contributing to the greatness of the new work, being only followers or journeymen. Nevertheless, in making art they will produce works that we can appreciate. So, apart from geniuses, there will be other accomplished artists who do not reach that height. What must we think of them?

It is difficult to *feel* moved by a painting of a fishing boat listing on a Spanish beach, its nets spilling over one edge; it's oars lying next to each other and protruding from inside the boat, propped against the gunwales; the seascape, a calm horizon behind, the sea a mute blue, the sky a glazed cyan. Nevertheless, one could discriminate between those who have a talent for the depiction of such scenes as opposed to those who do not. And so, there is a place for these journeyman artists who cater for a certain taste and who are accomplished in their professions as professional fine art painters. The difficulty we might feel is in the lack of imagination. On such matters, the poet, Carol Anne Duffy once remarked on clichés, 'You wouldn't want one of those sticking to your shoes.' For the architectural equivalent, there are too many examples of unthinking designs of buildings incorporating inane classical detail.

On the one hand, there are accomplished artists whose work does not rise much above proficiency. On the other, there are artists whose work not only lacks genius, but also fails as art. This could be because it cannot be accommodated within an art-kind and so it lacks criteria by which we can reasonably judge its success.

Kant warns us, whilst he is setting out the requirements for recognizing genius, that 'nonsense too can be original'. In the context of architecture, it is usually the functional aspect that prevents works from straying too far from reason. However, I am inclined to think that *House VI* is an exceptional case. At a research conference in London some years ago, I found myself complaining about Eisenman's project. I was duly rebuked. 'The reason you find it shocking', I was told, 'is that it doesn't conform to your preconceptions.' I replied, sincerely, that I didn't find the piece at all shocking. Rather, I found it silly. At that time, I wasn't consciously relying on a conception of architectural medium specificity. That was not possible, since I had no such conception of an architectural medium. However, nothing, as yet, has persuaded me otherwise.

Eisenman can design his buildings as he wants. The Franks' can commission buildings as they want. Nothing should stop them. Suzanne Frank claims that her family loves living in the house. Eisenman claims that it is obedient only to its own *internal* reasons. All I say is that I find neither rhyme nor reason to judge *House VI* beautiful *as a work of architecture*. I do not think Eisenman a master of his medium, although his work might give rise to interesting questions concerning it.

IV The bird and her place

Taking seriously my fellow delegate's reprimand sheds light on functionalism and mitigates Eisenman's stance. For Eisenman terms himself a 'post-functionalist' (Eisenman 1996). In so doing, he rejects affiliation with postmodernism, which he maintains is an impossible position to occupy, as modernism has yet to appear. He states that what we have witnessed, continually over the past five hundred years, the half millennium since the Renaissance, is humanism. He goes on to identify this with an anthropocentric metaphysics, which he regards as untenable.

'Form follows function', Louis Sullivan proclaimed, and the functionalists obligingly got in line. This, as often interpreted, is the aphorism that merely sustains the anthropocentricity of old; as is our wont, or so it is claimed; architectural form is determined by the use of the building.

However, Sullivan's slogan neither confirms nor confounds Kant's requirement that architecture must address the use for which a work is designed. Sullivan's functionalism is an attempt to place architecture in the realm of nature. That might sound odd to the modernist, especially one who thinks in terms of the programme as a determinant of the building. However, the aphorism appears in Sullivan's autobiography. Here is the detail. I quote, at length, Hanno-Walter Kruft's major work, *A History of Architectural Theory from Vitruvius to the Present*,

> Looking back on his partnership with Adler, [Sullivan] writes, in a moment of self-characterization in the third person, that it had been his aim at that time to realize the dream that he had long nourished, namely
>
> > to make an architecture that fitted its functions – a realistic architecture based on well defined utilitarian needs – that all practical demands of utility should be paramount as basis of planning and design …
>
> All architecture must be apprehended plastically; all conventional rigidity must be removed from it, so that it can serve a sensible purpose and not become oppressive. Then comes the important conclusion:
>
> > In this wise the forms under his [i.e. Sullivan's] hand would grow naturally out of the needs and express them frankly, and freshly. This meant … a formula he had evolved, through long contemplation of living things, namely that *form follows function.*
>
> The concept of function is central for Sullivan. He sees all forms of life as expressions of functions, and each function has its own form. Functions in Nature are 'powers' of life. For architecture this means that the function of a building must determine its organization and form. But this function is defined as the 'application to man's thought and deeds; to his inherent powers and the results of the application of these powers, mental, moral, physical … ' (Kruft 1994, 357).

To be sure, Kant insists that the use is paramount in our concern with the aesthetic ideas we encounter in works of architecture. However, the paramouncy of utility does not demand that 'all conventional rigidity' should be subtracted from the design. Whilst Kant thinks that architecture must be *seen* to serve a sensible purpose – how else could the *aesthetic* idea be communicated? – yet he does not take the stronger view that all 'conventional rigidity' has no place in the design. Thus, Kant's insistence on the purpose of the building being constituent of its *idea* does not entail that the building cannot demonstrate, in the aesthetic experience to which it gives rise, some other parallel image. (Perhaps we could think of examples of the corkscrew here – those novelty pieces of equipment, examples of which are fish, whose bodies extend as the cork is pulled, or a man's bow legs that splay as the cork is levered out.) We need not, therefore, follow Kruft's interpretation of Sullivan. Sullivan, as he describes himself, is of a view that is compatible with Kant's, even if not necessarily compliant to it.

So, Sullivan finds in nature the basis of his notion of function. However, whilst turning to nature as the source of form, he thinks of that nature as ours, and includes within its dimensions 'our thought and deeds'; our 'powers, mental, moral, physical'. We can think of architecture, that is, as arising out of our own nature. So, when Kant argues that architecture, unlike the other fine arts, is the art 'whose form does not have nature as its determining basis', he resists the view that architecture is representational. In essence, Sullivan's functionalism is compatible with Kant's view if we think of Sullivan making the claim that our nature is such as to structure our environment in terms of our mental, moral and physical powers.

The bird building her nest, the beaver her dam, the bee his hive, each puts her (or his) species at the centre of their activity. That is not a metaphysical stance taken up by these charming bits of nature unreflectively pursuing their humdrum lives. Could we not think of the anthropocentricity of the Renaissance as equally modest and sanction some form of functionalism accordingly? The Italian Renaissance used the *braccia* as a measure – the length of a man's arm. That's humanism. It does not entail a conception of the universe spinning about man. (Although, admittedly, that view of the world obtained back then.)

The *braccia's* contribution to architecture need not be abandoned on account of our metaphysical revisions. The bird finds her place in a nest assembled to accommodate her eggs, and then her chicks. Nests are the right size for the birds they accommodate. They are, of their nature, bird-centric. But to derive from that an ornithocentric metaphysics is for the birds. It is sophistry.

At least one strand of neo-classicism adopted formalist principles. Such buildings were neo-classical in detail, simple and symmetrical; and sometimes referred to as rationalist. This term indicates that, as opposed to the functionalism of the nest, hive and dam, organizational structures, geometric projections, symmetries and patterns overrode pragmatic concerns. However, our nature is to think rationally, and so geometry, symmetry and patterns are acceptable manifestations of our nature in architecture. Indeed, they might reasonably be thought to express our nature in architecture.

In Italy, one strand of modernism, neo-rationalism, set itself against the sterility and stifling conclusions of the functionalists. Giuseppe Terragni's *Casa Del Fascio* in Como is a beautiful example of this Italian sub-genre. It is unfortunately associated with Italy's flirtation with fascism. Terragni, himself a fascist, justified the building in terms of Mussolini's concept that 'Fascism is a glass house into which all can enter' (Colquhoun 2002, 185).

Post-functionalism with its sole adherent is not neo-rationalism. Nevertheless, in his comments on the American avant-gardist New York Five, Kenneth Frampton singles Terragni out as a major influence on Eisenman. Neo-rationalism is of the persuasion that function should be subordinated to architectural composition and invention. The geometries and patterns of the neo-structuralists are developed as independent structures governing the overall vision of the building. Its function is not denied but is accommodated within the more important conceptual grasp of the building as having quasi-autonomous design components.

Post-functionalism, by contrast, was developed in the heady atmosphere of University of Cambridge post-structuralist literary theory. (Structuralism and post-structuralist literary theory rely upon late nineteenth-century and twentieth-century linguistics applied to literature.) It was in the School of Architecture in Cambridge that Eisenman wrote up his doctoral thesis.

V Function reconsidered

The Functionalists appeared in Germany as part of the broader movement within and beyond the visual arts, *Neue Sachlichkeit* (New Objectivity). It was a modernist movement intent on realism after the Great War and was centred in Bauhaus Dessau. Its aims were focused on providing clean, healthy, modest dwellings for the communities. Walter Gropius, the first director of the school, designed its buildings according to the optimistic endeavours of the *Neue Sachlichkeit*: clean, affordable, healthy and enlightened, *functionalist*.

Colin Rowe introduced the New York Five in a catalogue essay. The five included Eisenman. In his dismissive passage concerning functionalism, designed to show in one paragraph what it was the five were setting themselves against, Rowe writes,

> When, in the late 1940s, modern architecture became established and institutionalized, necessarily, it lost something of its original meaning. Meaning, of course, it had never been supposed to possess. Theory and official exegesis had insisted that the modern building was absolutely without iconographic content, that it was no more than the illustration of a program, a direct expression of social purpose. Modern architecture, it was pronounced, was simply a rational approach to building; it was a logical derivative from functional and technological facts; and – at the last analysis – it should be regarded in these terms, as no more than the inevitable result of twentieth century circumstances.
>
> (Rowe 1998, 74)

It was against the *Neue Sachlichkeit* that Eisenman pitched his neo-avant-garde 'Post functionalism'.

Eisenman's furrow was ploughed in a different field from the neo-rationalists. His rejection of functionalism is born out of his

FIGURE 7.3 *Walter Gropius, Bauhaus, Dessau, Student Housing and Studios, 1925–6. © Spyrosdrakopoulos, 2014.*

thinking of architecture as language. As such he has been described as developing an internal syntax for architecture and of working within the semantics of architecture. In this he is not alone. Across the arts, first structural linguistics and then post-structuralism have had a strong influence. Suffice to say that Rowe's introductory paragraph intimates that meaning has replaced function; and so, the avant-garde architect must now regard the art of architecture as engaging with the 'languages' of the various arts, whilst, at the same time, developing and exploiting new 'ways of meaning' in architecture itself. For an assessment of the attempt to regard architecture as language, and its inevitable failure, see (Winters 2007, 61–91).

The devaluation of functionalism by both the neo-rationalists and the post-functionalist does not really address the point that Kant makes in the *Third Critique*. Kant does not suppose that the requirement to address purpose in a building prevents it from having iconographic content, or that it prescribes the illustration of a programme, or that it was logically entailed by functional and technological facts. It might, when fleshed out, claim that it is a direct expression of social purpose, but only insofar as that is true of any art. Certainly, it would claim that architecture, along with the rest of the fine arts, is a rational approach to making buildings under its own medium specificity.

VI Space, volume and pattern

As we noted in Chapter 4, there is only one space. It is boundless, and so shapeless. (It has no edges, and it can have none.) The phenomenology of being situated in space, amongst all things great and small, provides each of us with a unique perspective, gazing out upon its vastness. What we see in space are its many occupants related to each other and related to ourselves.

Since space is one and continuous, we cannot make space, we can only tinker about with its occupants. Architects do not make spaces, but their particular brand of tinkering makes objects contained within boundaries, which are volumetric. The boundaries define what is internal and what is external; and where those boundaries are pierced with window, door or other means of slipping between exterior and interior, we have liminal conditions.

These volumes designed by architects to manage our *Lebenswelt* are three-dimensional patterns, through which we move or rest and in which we otherwise take up occupancy. As patterns they determine our freedom. (This is the point that Langlands and Bell so beautifully demonstrate in their various pieces.) And it is the principal achievement of good architecture, that it provides for our freedom in such a way that we have reason to cherish the homes we inhabit. (I am using 'home' here in its broadest sense – returning us to Heidegger's sense of dwelling.)

VII Thinking through architecture

In Chapter 3, we looked at Alberti on lineaments and considered their relative independence of the building to which they nevertheless refer. In his essay on the translation of drawing to eventual building, Robin Evans addresses the state of architecture and its position in the schools (Evans 1997). The essay has a great deal to tell us about the medium of architecture, and he shows great wisdom in negotiating a peace between those who think the drawing has its own status as art ('paper architecture') and those who think of architecture as a more abstract pursuit. Both of these notions need some clarification.

In the first, he considers the idea that, alongside developments in painting and sculpture, the drawing itself becomes the work, since that is what architects *do*. So, the materiality of the medium insists that we take that as the *work*. However, that is more an analogy with Nelson Goodman's recommendation that we take the score to be the work of music. Both the architectural drawing and the musical score then assume a more important role than has traditionally been accorded. Since the analogy is strong, it is worth considering objections to Goodman's example. If the work of music is identified with the score, I must be able to experience the music in the score – presumably by reading it. However, there are folk that can experience music who cannot read scores. (I humbly admit I am one.) Moreover, the movement in the music is something *heard*, and not read. Tonality might be understood in the reading of a score (by those who can read), but its character is surely in what it is to hear tones as related. It is possible that we can hum a tune in our heads, if we can read music. However, 'hearing' a tune in one's head is not a case of hearing. (Recall our earlier concerns with Hume's 'faded impressions'.) Hence, a work of music is to be identified with a certain kind of experience, and reading a score is not commensurate with that experience. Otherwise we could hum tunes in our heads without bothering to attend concert performances.

By analogy, our experience of architecture, the great sense of beauty we feel in its embrace is only secondarily accessible to us through reading its drawings. (When it rains in Oxford Street, architectural drawings of Selfridges department store will not keep us warm and dry.) The altered definition of architecture in modernity, as Evans has it, cannot consist in the architectural drawing. If that option, let's call it the material identity option, needs refinement, we could push the drawing aside and identify the work as demanding the architect's direct involvement in the actual building. Either way, the work is to be considered as the unmediated product of the architect's hand.

The second option is diametrically opposed to this. This is to conceive of the work as communicated, transitive properties of the drawing. It is to conceive of the work as accessed by the drawing in its special status as engaging the architectural imagination. That special status can be seen by contrasting drawing as practised in Western art before modernism, where nature was the source of art's representation; and architecture, where the drawing precedes the work and is *logically* anterior to it.

Evans ends his essay with a call to arms. It is loud and clear,

> It would be possible, I think, to write a history of Western architecture that would have little to do with either style or signification, concentrating instead on the manner of working. A large part of this history would be concerned with the gap between drawing and building. In it the drawing would be considered not so much a work of art or a truck for pushing ideas from place to place, but as the locale of subterfuges and evasions that one way or another get round the enormous weight of convention that has always been architecture's greatest security and at the same time its greatest liability.
>
> (Evans 1997, 185–6)

That gap between drawing and building is envisioned by Alberti as a use of the imagination and his conception of the work of the architect as 'translating' the ideas he imagines into 'drawings', then having to adjust the drawings (and presumably, on occasion, adjust his ideas). He then 'passes' from drawings to 'models', where he finds other material deficiencies with which he has to contend; again adjusting the model and/or adjusting his ideas.

Evans' emphasis on the place of drawing is interesting for two reasons. The first is that, when we look at the history of architectural drawing, we meet with, almost without exception, frontality. That is, we regard the flat drawing as mapping onto some aspect of the building *front-on*. This is the case not just with elevations, but also with plans and sections. The idea that such projective drawings conform to or confirm a Cartesian three-dimensional grid need not confine the architect to box-like orthogonal structures. Any point in space can be precisely located in an x, y, z (height, width and depth) notation.

Secondly, and relatedly, the movement forward and backward, between drawing and building (built, modelled or imagined) returns us to Aristotle's thought that we can learn about an object from its line drawings. In architecture we learn about the building from its lineaments. Hence, part of our appreciation of architecture relies upon introjection from the buildings to these outlines (drawn or imagined).

Down to the smallest scale, the architect thinks through the design and arrives at a suitable piece of detail – detail that will be the result of an overall conception of the building; and that will, in turn, contribute to that conception. It is this conception of architecture that Muñoz Molina's fictional architect Ignacio Abel so well exemplifies. It also gives strength to our consideration of Trevor Dannatt's thumb groove on the banister at the Royal Festival Hall.

So much for the process, with the engagement of the imagination through drawing and model-making, of making architecture. The finished building will be an accomplishment of the architect, even as it is built by craftsmen and other experts. The work of architecture as an art is that building we inhabit and appreciate as an art, in accordance with these constraints.

The work will not stand or fall on whether the architect is aligned to the correct epistemology or metaphysics. It will be judged, however, on the richness of experience engaging thought concerning the nature of our accommodation in a world to which we must be adjusted.

8

The scale of the tasks

I Large (the city)

The Situationist International (SI) – lauded and reviled in equal measure, according to the leaning of the laudator or reviler – politicized the pleasurable saunter of the nineteenth-century *flâneur*. Innocent, if not perfectly so, the *flâneur*, usually a poet, usually a man, always a dandy, would saunter about Paris, enjoying his promenade; occasionally stopping at a café for a drink, looking at his fellow denizens, whilst being looked at, in turn, in the city of light. What we know of him is that he would write notes recording observations and perfecting them into poems or short stories as was his wont. Charles Baudelaire regarded the *flâneur* as a 'gentleman stroller of city streets', seeing his role as contributing to, whilst observing and understanding, the city through which he dawdled. *Paris Spleen*, first published in 1869, a selection of fifty prose poems, provides testimony (Baudelaire 2021).

Guy Debord, a twentieth-century Marxist philosopher, represented the *Lettrist International* (a group of poets, philosophers and artists) at the inaugural meeting of The Situationist International, at Cosio d'Arroscia (Imperia), Italy in July 1957. Others in attendance were the International Movement for an Imaginist Bauhaus and The London Psychogeographical Association. The SI comprised Dadaists, Surrealists and members of European modern art group CoBrA. Debord was a main theorist and is responsible for bringing his concept of the *dérive* from the *Lettrists*, with whom he was previously involved.

The *dérive* is a method developed to discover the life of those who live in the city – to reveal itself in the creation of new situations. To undertake a *dérive*, it is the responsibility of the agent to seek out new routes through the city, to find their attractions and to exploit these attractions by engaging with circumstances thrown up. It is an exhortation to set about having new experiences by walking the city. In this it is also a rejection of the everyday and the humdrum existence foisted upon us by utilitarian demands.

The concept has been a major influence in contemporary art and is much used in architecture school to sensitize students to the nature of the city. As Loli Waxman puts it,

> The average person, [Debord] claimed, exerts no control over his or her everyday life, living it passively and under various kinds of unquestioned, utilitarian obligations: to work and to consume foremost among them. Meanwhile these lives grow increasingly atomized and privatized (…) separating banal office jobs in the city from isolated prefab homes in the suburbs via lengthy, dull commutes on the metro.
>
> (Waxman 2017, 89)

Here is a case of quite openly rejecting functionalism as a stultifying method of inhabiting the city. However, it must not go unremarked that this criticism of the way a life is prosecuted need not be an upshot of Kant's claim that buildings are essentially functional.

In the first issue of the *Situationist International,* English artist, Ralph Rumney, living in Paris, wrote a piece in which he included a map of the daily travels of a Paris student. It was a drawn record and consists mainly in a triangle. The route is from home to university to piano lesson to home. This map was itself an argument that the city is not being experienced, and that her daily travels were merely passages of time spent between the three locations. The city, under SI's conception, is a magnificent collection of opportunities. It is this city with which we are urged to become engaged.

From an architectural point of view, the large scale of the city demands an occupation that can only take place over extended periods of time. It is large in scale and we must try to understand it as a series of optional locations, in which we might pursue one ambition or another. However, it is a context into which the architect must realize her building as a component part. In this, it appears as though a concrete example of Eliot's history of an art. For the insertion of a new building changes the entire city, 'if ever so slightly', and the ripples diminish as we venture further to the edges of the city. It has most consequence upon its immediate neighbours, but this does not mitigate its influence on the furthest flung of the city's limits.

In the city there are parks and squares and places of communal gathering. These are the places in which we meet for festivities, both formal and informal. The village green is traditionally the venue for the annual cricket match, held between the squire's manor house and its staff, and the village outside. It is both a grudge match and a coming together of the village in its circumscribed collective. After the match the pub on the green will host the celebration and commiseration. The pub league is a football competition that pits bar against bar, where old lags can toddle about in memory of their better days. Again, the home team's pub will provide sandwiches and the first round of drinks.

From the village to the city, where bars are focused on more specialized communities. The French House in Soho, London, was at one time the exiled headquarters of the Free French, where General de Gaulle met with his compatriots on a regular basis in an upstairs room. The bar only serves half-pints of beer and up until his departure, the landlord, Gaston Berlement, served glasses of absinthe to regulars on Sunday lunchtimes. It is a bar frequented by writers and artists, journalists and those from the local sex trade, as well as art and architecture students.

In the city are the places of social connection, perhaps the most notable of which is the bar. Bars are places to meet and turn aside from the daily commerce that draws its participants. To turn away from, even momentarily, is to breathe a different air. It is here we are intoxicated in the company of our kind and where we can hold forth and argue about the passions of our lives, rather than glue ourselves onto the tedium of the mechanical world. The bar is an opportunity for freedom both within and beyond reason. Stories of friends and acquaintances who have sauntered away from the path of reason amuse us, and those same stories of mere acquaintances are enough to turn them into friends.

The bar is a spiritual home for those without myths to comfort them, and a bar's architecture has the profundity of home. The English refer to these places as public houses, where we can be both public and yet belong, as if in our own house. In a bar is a collection of individuals with which to be reckoned. Pubs are places where we get drunk; we make friends in them; we lose friends in them; we fall in love in them; we do the crossword in them; we eat their humble fare in them and we slowly change our minds in them. We can, of course, in reckless moments, lose our dignity in them, lose our minds in them. We can do and say things we shall regret in them, and we can be told we must never return to them. (And yet we do.) Life, however, that most important feature of an aesthetic pursuit, would be very much duller without them. (This, I take to be the point of the SI's *dérive.*) Raymond Chandler's Philip Marlowe, commiserating with Lennox, a reformed alcoholic, says to him something like, 'You'd better get used to softer sounds and paler colours.'

A bar is part of the architecture of life; it is a room within it, closed off from the worldly requirements of commerce and other such squalor. It is the sitting room of the city. You wander round the city and more or less every corner is a sitting room. Francis Ford Coppola's biopic of beat poet, Charles Bukowski, *Barfly*, has a series of opening shots of small bars around Los Angeles. They are, each of them, beautiful little sanctuaries. Once inside a bar, we step out of it only into the functional tedium, the wretched world of efficiency and accountability. The bar is a sacred space for the atheist, a place where we are forgiven our sins even as we commit them. A bar is a place for the human heart. It is, all things considered, a dysfunctional place; a home, even for those 'unhomed' by a melancholy fetched in on Bohemian swells of salted water. Perhaps it is the salted water that induces thirst.

For those who do not understand the bar as their natural place of rest or relaxation, I ask that they might think by analogy of another place in which to find shelter from the kind of storm from which the bar protects. The coffee house is currently enjoying favour; the greasy-spoon (diner) perhaps; the library tea-room or the senior and junior common rooms. Somewhere immune from the agents in search of profit and accumulation. A bar is somewhere such agents can neither irritate or intimidate us. It is a place, however brief, of rest and recreation.

Episodic restful recreation is one thing – after which, freshened, we are ready to face the inanities of life. Rest is part of the natural rhythm of life and thus, it is enjoyed. Eternal rest is quite another. Its architecture, suitably morbid. Bars are for the living. What of the dead? Their cities, the great cemeteries of the world, are sombre, lifeless. Why do we perisist in our visits to those departed? We respect the dead and must not speak ill of them. (The 'we' in these last two sentences refers to humanity past and present. Respect for the dead is demanded. It is the wont of humanity at large, the *sensus communis*, to *feel* in awe of the dead.)

II Cities of the dead

> Hegra's largest tomb, measuring about 72 feet tall, is the monolithic Tomb of Lihyan Son of Kuza, sometimes called Qasr al-Farid, meaning the 'Lonely Castle' in English, because of its distant position in relation to the other tombs. It was left unfinished, with rough, unsmoothed chisel marks skirting its lower third. A few tombs were abandoned mid-construction for unclear reasons. The deserted work at Tomb 46 shows most clearly how the Nabataeans built from top to bottom, with only the stepped 'crown' visible above an uncut cliffside. Both the Tomb of Lihyan Son of Kuza and Tomb 46 have short inscriptions, designating them for specific families.
>
> (Keith 2020)

A 'lonely castle' indeed. Who lives there? The idea of a city of the dead is an oxymoron. Cities are alive, as heads are sometimes 'alive' with lice, or sewers with vermin. There is a scene in Carol Reed's 1949 film adaptation of Graham Greene's, *The Third Man*, in which Harry Lime (a Black marketeer) asks Holly Martins (visiting from the moral high ground) something like, 'Look down there. Would you really feel any pity if one of those dots [the multitude at whom they look down from the top of the big wheel in Vienna] were to stop moving; for ever?' The story, of course, is written by a recently converted Roman Catholic. The final scene sees Lime trapped in the city's sewer system, unable to reach the streets above, looking up at the artificial light of the city from the shadows of his interior life. Cities remind us of what we are.

The now-expired Colony Room Club in Soho was a small oasis in London, frequented by artists, writers, sex workers, theatrical types and Soho habitués; where the filthy carpet would stick to your

FIGURE 8.1 Tomb of Lihyan, Son of Kusa, *Hegra, Saudi Arabia, 3rd–2nd Century BC. © Ahmad AlHasanat, 2017.*

feet as you approached the bar, usually to engage in an exchange of unpleasantries before you were served. On one afternoon, a member brought in a guest who asked in all innocence, 'What's that smell?' Without looking up another member muttered, 'Failure'. The city is a home for the cynic and her bitter humour.

And yet, we visit the graves of the dead. Père Lachaise Cemetery in Paris houses great artists and writers from Paris and further afield. Architecture, we might think, gains its aesthetic dimension from our sense of what it is to inhabit a space. It is beautiful, but what makes it beautiful is the *thought* of its accommodating our unfolding lives. Strictly speaking no-one is buried in a cemetery, since all that gets buried are mortal remains. The dead, as it were, are the dearly departed. What, then, must we think about funerary architecture of the cemetery?

One thing to notice is the predominance of classical details. Death, we might suppose, requires solemnity and a sense of the eternal. Classicism is an apt reminder that we are continuous with antiquity, from whence derives our civilization. Pére Lachaise is littered with examples of these classical ædicules; and strange little temples they are, usually about the size of Gilbert Scott's telephone booth we came across in Chapter 1. (Interestingly, it was John Soane's design for his and his wife's grave in St Pancras Cemetery in London, that Scott took as a template for the booth.)

There are other more modern graves in the cemetery, more fitting for those whose remnant traces are there interred. Gerda Taro, the photo-journalist who volunteered to fight fascism in the Spanish Civil War is buried there; as is Paul Elouard, the Dadaist, later Surrealist, poet. They are both interred at the far corner of the cemetery – a pocket of the cemetery that has Gertrude Stein and Oscar Wilde within stumbling distance. I wonder if Taro, Stein and Elouard knew each other. Stein and Elouard must have done, since both were close friends of Picasso; and Paris was such a small place for bohemians just before the war.

FIGURE 8.2 *Tomb of Gerda Taro, Père Lachaise Cemetery, Paris, 2019. Photograph by Edward Winters.*

Well, even if Oscar Wilde regards them as newcomers, they are all neighbours now. Only they are not, and for the reason set out above. They do not *inhabit* the cemetery.

Why, then, drift around the cemetery, looking for Gerda Taro's tomb, eager to stand at the foot of a grave of one whom we have admired but never met? It is a puzzle: a phenomenological puzzle. (Recall that when Sartre and Beauvoir met up with Aron in the Bec-de-Gaz bar in Montparnasse, Aron advised his friends, 'if you are a phenomenologist, you can talk about this cocktail and make philosophy out of it'?)

Is mourning utterly irrational? When we mourn, we are connecting ourselves to a community of souls, each of whom commands respect. Traditions, customs and enshrined values include both dead and alive; and, indeed, those who are yet to be. The *sensus communis* stretches backwards and forwards, as well as outwards from a central ego.

We have duties to ourselves but also to the dead, and to the unborn. That is why it was so important to have pardoned Oscar Wilde under the 'Turin Law' (2017) for his so-called 'gross indecency'.

When we regard infants, we do so with respect for them as persons, even when they are too young to have grasped reason. We look upon them, not as persons, capable of making decisions or of being fully responsible for their actions, but as persons *in potentia*. That is, we come to regard them as future persons who will have reason and will be culpable for their actions. As such we recognize duties towards them.

Is this a way of re-interpreting our responses to the dead? They are no longer persons, but they demand our respect precisely because they once were. We do not live with the dead but we abide by them, as they abide with us. When I stand beside the tomb of Gerda Taro, I am brought to silence, not by her presence, but by her abiding memory.

The tomb makes sacred a life now ended and accounted for. I may put flowers on her grave as a symbol of my respect. She is no longer a person but the life she led deserves enduring respect, even though I know her only through testimony. Taro (real name, Gerta Pohorylle) moved to Paris in 1934, where she met Hungarian photo-journalist, Endre Ernő Friedmann.

Both were Jewish and each was fleeing oppression from their respective homelands. Taro had already been arrested in Germany for distributing anti-fascist literature. The two invented an American photo-journalist, Robert Capa, whose work they were able to sell for three times the going rate, Americans being granted such kudos. They were soon discovered but by then their work had become so successful it didn't matter. Friedman became Capa, and the pair went to cover the Republican side of the Spanish Civil War.

Taro met her death in a tragic accident whilst returning from the front at the battle of Brunete. It was a sad end, a stupid end, as stupid as war itself. It was a pitiful end to such a courageous, reckless, wonderful life. She was beautiful, too. Perhaps that shouldn't affect my response, but it does. It ended thus,

> Taro had ignored warnings from Capa and others to stay away from the frontline at one of the most dangerous moments in the war and, having used up all her film, had hitched a ride on the running boards of a general's car that was being used to ferry the injured. As they were strafed by German aircraft supporting Franco's troops near Villanueva de la Cañada, an out-of-control tank from the republican army ran into them and she was mortally wounded in the stomach.
>
> (Tremlett 2018)

Why visit her tomb? My visit to her grave is not a visit to her home, but it is a visit to her abode. In cemeteries, the dead abide. In standing silently beside the graves, we mourn their passing, even as we abide with them.

This, I hope, gives a third dimension to the idea of a *sensus communis*. It connects us, as photographs connect us; and as the rugs of the Navajo women connect the tribe through its history. There is good *reason* to visit the cemetery. There we find an architecture that provides abode, even for the dead.

Think of the contribution that architecture makes to literature and cinema. The city in film is often dark so that we think of the city at night, its avenues of crime mapping onto the avenues of our imagination. In the novel we inhabit the city, then a room, then a particular upholstered chair in which we sat waiting; or we sit in a car looking through a windshield as its wipers squeak to and fro, the scene blurring and clearing in monotonous rhythm with the soundtrack. We remember cities and when we do so, our imaginations are enlivened by their vivacity; as if our mental imagery reaches out to the city itself.

> There are cities that remain mere distant visual images when remembered, and cities that are remembered in all their vivacity. The memory re-evokes the delightful city with all its sounds and smells and variations of light and shade. I can even choose whether to walk on the sunny side or the shaded side of the street in the pleasurable city of my remembrance. The real measure of the qualities of a city is whether one can imagine falling in love with it.
> (Pallasmaa 2012, 75)

The city and the cemetery: I was once walking with the poet and translator Michael Sullivan. We were looking at some old Hugenot weavers' houses just off the Commercial Road near Aldgate in the East End of London. A car pulled up and a man shouted from the driver's seat. A woman in one of the houses we were looking at threw up the window and shouted down to the driver, 'Where y' goin'? 'Cemetery. Yer' comin?' 'I don' wanna go cemetery' she shouted down and closed the window. The car drove off. Sullivan turned to me and said 'None of us wanna go cemetery'; so we walked on to a bar in Whitechapel.

III Small *(the details)*

Everyday aesthetics brings home to us the small epiphanies: beer caps, decorated with the suits of playing cards, in the dust outside a bar in small town Mexico; a silver button-hole flower holder on an old man's lapel; accessories after the fact. Arne Jacobsen, architect of St Catherines College Oxford, designed the cutlery for the refectory. When looking at the city, the plan has to fit with all the infrastructural consequences of putting a building *here*. At the other extreme, the architect must confront the devil in the detail. Casati and Varsi pointed to these extremes, 'millimeters to kilometers': from the detail to the city.

In Muñoz Molina's novel, Ignacio Abel recalls his fictional professor at the Bauhaus, who would fetch his brief case into the lecture hall and then proceed, one by one, to remove its contents:

> Professor Rossman was like a peddler of the most vulgar, most improbable things. He lectured as easily on the practical virtues of a spoon's curvature as on the exquisite visual rhythms of the radii of a bicycle wheel in motion. Other professors at the School proselytised for the new, while Professor Rossman revealed the innovation and sophistication that remain hidden and yet produce results in what has always existed. He would clear the middle of the table, place on it a top he'd bought on his way to the School from some children playing in the street, start it twirling with an abrupt, skilled gesture, and watch it spin, as dazzled as if he were witnessing the rotation of a heavenly body. 'Invent something like this,' he challenged the students with a smile. 'Invent the top, or the spoon, or the pencil. Invent the book that can be carried in a pocket and contains the *Iliad* or Goethe's *Faust*. Invent the match, the jug handle, the scale, the carpenter's folding ruler, the sewing needle, the scissors. Perfect the wheel or the fountain pen. Think of the time when some of these things didn't exist.' Then he looked at his wristwatch – he was enthusiastic about this new gadget, which had appeared, according to him, amongst British officers during the war – picked up his things, placed his lunatic inventor's or junkman's objects back in his briefcase, filled his pockets with them, and dismissed the class with a nod and a mock military click of his heels.
>
> (Muñoz Molina 2015, 59–60)

It is a very fine passage that takes us into the momentous importance of little things. It also slides easily between the city (the children playing in the street from whom he bought the top) and the spoon or the handle of a jug. In the description of the Colony Room Club, the stickiness and the smell of the carpet are small details that colour the experience of diving into a bar from the swirling uncontrollable torrents of the city outside. The city gives us these extremes. The details are what bind us into the city. The feel of a doorhandle, the resistance of the door as we push our way through into the bar.

9

Concluding remarks

I Paris cafés

There is a bar in Paris with a notice which proudly proclaims, 'Ernest Hemingway did not drink here'. Paris is full of delightful bars, and, in no small way, this bar makes its contribution. I simply cannot remember its name or location, but I think I enjoyed the visit. Ian Nairn, the architectural critic, writes,

> As a person who drinks a lot and can't bear either pretensions or possessiveness, I look for a shabby but clean hotel and a restaurant where the menu is written up daily in near-illegible purple ink.
>
> (Nairn 2017, 2)

This sentence is embossed on the hard cover of the book, and it stands synecdochically not just for the rest of the book, but for Paris as experienced by Nairn. You get the feel of the city from his beautiful prose. As a guide, he puts you in a frame of mind.

A friend once observed that Paris is dense, meaning that within the *Périférique* you are in Paris. You simply walk out of your door and you are there. This makes walking Paris a constant pleasure and an often-aimless pursuit. You don't have to get anywhere.

Nairn gets quite political about it,

> It doesn't matter much which boulevard you choose, in this homogenous city, cracked open by Hausmann to provide fields of fire in case of insurrection – the lion has eaten the trainer. The smartest boulevards have trees and don't go anywhere (...) But

> every boulevard has its café, nests of insurgence: broad awnings, tables that rarely fill up completely, always a place to sit down and watch the world go by. The basic vacuity of the avenues turns out to be an entrance ticket to liberation. For the café-dweller, quietly sipping Slavia or Kronenbourg, it seems to be all freedom and no rules. The rules, in fact, have been forgotten, and now there are just people, enjoying the amplitude and oblivious of nineteenth-century military techniques. Hard luck, Baron H.: game, set and match to the rabble.
>
> (Nairn 2017, 9)

In Chapter 8, we looked at our response to the city, and we considered the importance placed upon our experience of the city to the Situationist International. The relationship between spectator and architect is crucial, as it was argued that in coming to form an architectural intention, it is essential that the architect occupy the position of the spectator in order to engage her task.

Here is architectural theorist and Cambridge professor, Dalibor Vesely, on the French café,

> If we look closely at a concrete example – a French café, for instance – it is obvious that its essential nature is only partly revealed in its visible appearance; for the most part that essence is hidden in the field of references to the social and cultural life related to the place (…) Its representational, ontological structure can be grasped through a preunderstanding that is based on our familiarity with what is being studied and with a segment of the world to which it belongs. Preunderstanding in this case is a layered experience of the world, acquired through our involvement in the events of everyday life. The identity of the French café is to a great extent defined by the café's institutional nature, rooted in the habits, customs, and rituals of French life (…) The visible 'text' of the café reveals certain common, deep characteristics, such as its location, its relation to the life of the street, its transparency of enclosure, a certain degree of theatricality (…), an ambiguity of inside and outside expressed not only in the transparency of enclosure but also in the café's typical furniture, and so on. These are only some of the characteristics that contribute to the identity and meaning of the French café as a culturally distinct typical situation.
>
> (Vesely 2006, 77–9)

Vesely was a follower of Hans-Georg Gadamer, himself a student of Heidegger. Vesely taught at University of Essex on the prestigious graduate programme, whose students included Daniel Liberskind, Robin Evans and David Leatherbarrow. He was recruited to teach on the graduate programme at Cambridge by Colin St John Wilson. A proponent of the continental phenomenological school, he helped to shape architectural theory internationally.

Nevertheless, the quotation above encounters a number of difficulties. The first is that it is unclear, unless Vesely has some theory of innocence in perception, why it is that the field of references is 'hidden'. Why can't we say that the visible world is saturated by concepts, as we did in Chapter 4, where Kant's manifold of perception regarded the role of imagination as bringing sensibility (intuitions) under concepts? So thinking, we could say that the 'café's institutional nature, rooted in the habits, customs, and rituals of French life,' is *apparent* in the experience we have of (and in) the café. This would still require that we attend to the *Lebenswelt* in our appreciation of what Vesely terms the 'situation'. Otherwise, Vesely's 'preunderstanding' is in danger of slipping out of our *experiential* grasp. Moreover, by restricting perception in the manner he does, Vesely throws understanding back onto a linguistic footing that other phenomenologists might want to resist.

If we wish to insist that perception is shot through with conceptual thought – that perception is conceptual throughout – we can still make room for aesthetic ideas by regarding these as both imaginative and indeterminate. In Chapter 5, we looked at Kant's idea of the 'free play of imagination' and we saw how that permitted the imagination to deliberately mis-apply concepts to sensations (intuitions). Freed from the duty imagination has in the perceptual process, it can entertain contents it knows do not obtain. Thus, we can see the clouds as faces of angry gods.

Kant's conception of fine art as a means of *communication* resists conceptual assimilation. The 'aesthetic idea' that each fine art is able to convey lies beyond determinate conceptual grasp. As Kant puts it,

> An *aesthetic idea* cannot become cognition because it is an *intuition* (of the imagination) for which an adequate concept can never be found. A *rational idea* can never become cognition because it contains a *concept* (of the supersensible) for which no adequate intuition can ever be given.

> I think we may call aesthetic ideas *unexpoundable* presentations of the imagination, and rational ideas *indemonstrable* concepts of reason.
>
> (Kant 1987, 342)

What this technical distinction permits is a field of rational activity, in which we are able to engage and in which we find aesthetic value. We both understand aesthetic ideas, and, in their apprehension, we are moved to *feelings* that appropriately secure our delight in their object as encountered. To attempt to fit that into a cognitive model is to misplace the aesthetic, and to misconstrue that which aesthetic ideas communicate.

In both painting and architectural theory, there is considerable confusion over Kant's views of beauty and its place in human affairs. Clement Greenberg, the theorist whose views were taken up by the American abstract expressionists, and one of the editors of *The Partisan Review* who gave Beauvoir such a difficult time on her visit to America, developed his idea about flat painting and his concomitant rejection of figuration out of his misapprehension of Kant's aesthetics (Greenberg 1995). For Greenberg, Kant's conception of pure beauty was to form the basis of formalism in painting. That ignored Kant's writing on the fine arts. It also ignored Kant's writing on the phenomenon of colour. (Kant thought colour was not a formal property of painting but was merely charm.)

II Function and medium (again)

We saw that Gordon Graham, interpreting architecture as a craft, disregarded architecture as a fine art, precisely because it has utility. So, too, does architectural historian and theorist, Adrian Forty. In his *Words and Buildings: A vocabulary of Modern Architecture*, he time and again misrepresents Kant.

Glenn Parsons, the analytical philosopher, puts the modernists' notion of function rather bluntly, before going on to write that it cannot be sustained: 'According to the Modernist view, aesthetic, mediating and expressive aspects need not be brought into the Design problem: it is a purely functional one' (Parsons 2016, 103).

However, Forty, in his book, provides five different readings of function. These are:

> 1 As a mathematical metaphor – a critique of the classical system of ornament.
>
> 2 As a biological metaphor, descriptive of the purposes of the parts of the construction relative to each other and to the whole.
>
> 3 As a biological metaphor within the 'organic' theory of form.
>
> 4 'Function' meaning 'Use'.
>
> 5 'Functional' as the translation of the German words '*sachlich*', '*zweckmässig*', '*funktionell*'. (Forty 2004, 174–80)

Given the sauce of the slogan, 'Form follows function', we can surmise that Louis Sullivan took it to be a biological metaphor in the sense of 3 above.

The fourth conception of functionalism was lampooned by Scruton in his *The Aesthetics of Architecture* (Scruton 2002). As early as page 7, he writes of crude functionalism that it was a theory 'as Theophile Gautier once pointed out, [that] has the consequence that the perfection of the water closet is the perfection to which all architecture aspires'. The view is not ridiculous, however. For water closets are designed objects and, indeed, have much of architectural importance in their conception: privacy and its corollary, exclusion, for two. Public lavatories are to be thought out in terms of modesty, privacy and exclusion. How does the architect reconcile publicity with privacy? It's an interesting problem. But why should *urinoirs* not be regarded as works of architecture alongside other buildings? It is a feature of what we are, mortal things with natural lives, that we need such facilities as water closets; especially if we are to spend so much time in bars.

In respect to 4 above, Forty takes functionalism to contravene Kant's prescription that pure beauty involves no concept.

> [A] difficulty under which architectural modernists laboured in their wish to make architecture an art that represented the 'social' was the longstanding exclusion of anything to do with use from the category of the aesthetic. Ever since Kant in *The*

> *Critique of Judgment* of 1794 first established the modern concept of the aesthetic as a distinct class of human perception, the purpose and utility of things were declared to lie outside aesthetic judgment.
>
> (Forty 2004, 105)

We have seen, however, that Kant does not regard the fine arts as examples of pure beauty; rather, he accords them a special place

FIGURE 9.1 *Charles Marville,* Urinoir en fonte à 2 stalles écran, Chaussée de la Muette, c. *1865, photograph, Public Domain, via Wikimedia Commons.*

within the realm of dependent beauties. Kant even goes so far as to write, as was noted above, that a thing, 'is fine art if its purpose is that the pleasure should accompany presentations that are *ways of cognizing*' (Kant 1987, 172).

III The streets of Paris

In the last chapter, we looked at the scale of the city and at the idea of experiencing the city by walking through it. Here is the story of a surrealist walk through Paris, as provided by Lori Waxman's book,

> In the spring of 1953, a group of friends set out to attend an opening [of a surrealist exhibition] in the bohemian Paris neighborhood of Saint-Germain-des-Prés (...) Their walk to the gallery did not end with complimentary glasses of wine and fancy small talk in front of strange, precious canvases but with repartee of an entirely different order, the kind made when one is brought into the local police station for drunken misconduct. They turned what should have been a brief dash into a marauding adventure with visits to some two dozen bars, where they became progressively drunker thanks to the Legros cocktails – a noxious concoction of pastis and rum – they consumed at every stop.
>
> Landing in jail that night probably did not surprise the friends, though it might have occurred earlier in the evening and for slightly different reasons than expected – they'd set out on their excursion with the intention of disrupting the opening. They loathed what Surrealism had become.
>
> (Waxman 2017, 85)

The group of friends were members of the *Lettrist International.* Among them for this evening was Debord, the political theorist who was to be a founder member of the Situationist International. Debord was influential in making a bridge between politics and art. The walk they took that evening was itself an instance of the *dérive.* Thirty years earlier, Breton, who curated the show which the group failed to disrupt, had been on a walk as a Dadaist event. That walk began in the Bar Cyrano where Breton often drank with fellow artists.

FIGURE 9.2 *Contemporary poet and playwright, Sam Kastin, at the Bar Cyrano, Paris, 2019. Photograph by Edward Winters.*

Bars and streets, politics and art, belong in the city. In the Bar Cyrano during a wander through the streets from Place du Clichy to Shakespeare and Co bookshop on the Left Bank, I look at poet Sam Kastin and muse, 'This is where it happened. This is where it is happening. This is where it will happen.' In so thinking, a whole culture is opened up in front of me, so to speak. Kastin and I are in one of Vesely's Paris Cafés, sipping one of Nairn's beers, walking close to the walk the Dadaists took to *St Julien le Pauvre* in 1921. (It is on the next block from Shakespeare & Co.)

Evans spoke of the architectural drawing being the site of 'subterfuges and evasions that one way or another get round the enormous weight of convention' that weighs down the subject of architecture. The SI painted slogans around the streets of Paris as provocations: '*Sous les pavés, la plage!*' ('Beneath the street, the beach!'), read one such. Paris is a beautiful city in which these interventions are contributions to that beauty. Beneath the cobbles, indeed, is the sand in which they are embedded.

FIGURE 9.3 Beneath the Street, the Beach, *2019. Photograph of cobbles embedded in sand at Porte Saint Denis, Paris, by Edward Winters.*

Street-fighting against the authorities in Paris has for ages called upon the streets' small cobbles being 'unbeached' and hurled at the representatives of authority: the police or the military. The SI, like the Lettrists before them, and like the delinquent youth that followed them, were periodically called to riot in this city. Romantically, the city is a youthful place but need not be seen as quite so turbulent. The city is restless. It is a neon lit spectacle of taxis and nightclubs, jazz and cocktails and Gaulloises-smoke-filled rooms engaging fierce cultural debate. You can smell the night in Paris.

This section of the chapter is vindicated by Aron's sipping an apricot cocktail and demanding that we make philosophy out of it. It is, as it were, justified by appeal to the *Lebenswelt*. Life in the city is in and amongst architecture. In this the architectural theorists who seek a poetry of architecture are right.

IV Putting others first

The *Lebenswelt*, insofar as it is the experienced world in which we shape our lives, makes its own demands; and in this it is humanist in outlook – and rightly so. Philosophy, as pursued by Kant and at least some of his followers, stops short of making claims about the introspective nature of phenomenology. Self-certainty, in as much as we can make sense of it, relies for its ground on all manner of other certainties. Whilst this may seem pre-philosophically counter-intuitive, we must not let that overrule the good sense of Kant's insertion of 'The Refutation of Idealism', in his second edition of *The Critique of Pure Reason.* It is there that Kant recasts his argument that our knowledge of the external world is immediate, and that only *through* this knowledge am I able to secure the knowledge of an interior world. In this refutation he has in mind both René Descartes' Cogito argument (I think therefore I am) and Bishop Berkeley's 'immaterialism' (the argument that there are no material objects. There are only ideas in minds). Both Descartes and Berkeley take first person perspective, introspection, as the surest basis of knowledge. As Kant further explains his proof in note 1 (of 3),

> Certainly, the representation 'I am', which expresses the consciousness that can accompany any thought, immediately includes in itself the existence of a subject; but it does not so include any *knowledge* of that subject, and therefore also no empirical knowledge, that is, no experience of it. For this requires, in addition to the thought of something existing, also intuition, and in this case inner intuition, in respect of which, that is, of time, the subject must be determined. But in order to so determine it, outer objects are quite indispensable; and it therefore follows that inner experience is itself possible only mediately, and only through outer experience.
>
> (Kant 1964, B277)

In note 3, Kant writes that it is a 'fact that the existence of outer things is required for the possibility of a determinate consciousness of the self'. This refutation does not disprove phenomenology, but it does place constraints upon how we must frame the *Lebenswelt.*

'I' must think of myself only through the existence of an external world made up of 'others', and of a world of external objects in which I take up occupancy. Indeed, the phenomenology of such an external world is the only guarantee of the possibility of an internal world. The shape of that external world is given as *life* within the furniture of the world: its architecture.

V The medium (for the last time)

The medium for a fine art is to be specified by the way in which the imagination of the artist is engaged with the material of the work. This engagement of the artist's imagination relies upon her learned ability to see and understand the making of works in the history of her medium. Thus, in undertaking the role of the spectator, she comes to an understanding of what kind of work is required.

In the case of the architect, this conception of the work is illustrated by the fictional Abel: by the translations from Alberti's imagination into drawing, from drawing into model, and then back to drawing as instruction to build; and by Evans' disquisition on the centrality of drawing in the work of the architect.

Lopes has argued, convincingly, that the buck passing theory requires the fine arts to be identified by means of their medium specificity. Hence, the problem we have been dealing with is to provide such a medium-specific characterization of works of architecture that will, thereby, secure their status as works of fine art.

Earlier we looked at Wollheim's account of the medium of painting, in the hope that getting clear about the exploitation in that art might shed light upon or, more optimistically, serve as an analogue for the medium of architecture. However, it might be argued that, whereas the application of paint to a flat surface in order to develop representational content explains the medium through its exploitation of properties of the paint-as-applied, the functionality of architecture makes plain the process of building and its use is, thereby, transparent. Its functionality wears its practicality on its face. It might seem there is no analogous gap between built form and function, or between built form and the practical uses to which we put the building, with the proposed analogue of the activity of painting and the appearance of the gods at play, or a silver tray of fruit beside a bottle of wine, or a boat tossed about in a wild and threatening seascape.

Graham, in his search for a secular architecture that might yet be enchanted, supposes that pre-enlightenment architecture had religion to provide enchantment. Thus, the place of worship was seen to be an example of architecture *par excellence*. In our secular times, modern-day houses of parliaments, law courts, palaces, national galleries and museums are proposed as possible buildings that might achieve 'architecturehood'. He goes on to argue that art galleries – the Guggenheim in Bilbao by Frank Gehry, or Tate Modern in London by Herzog and de Meuron, or the Nelson-Atkins Museum of Art, Henry Block Building in Kansas City by Steven Holl, for instance – in declaring their exhibitions and holdings to be the kind of thing that one returns to, are a modern-day equivalent of the temple. They house what we hold dear.

That, however, sets aside as 'mere building' the housing that accommodates us and forms our homes. It turns architecture into some grand art that is built to make grand declarations. It runs against Kant granting the work of the cabinet-maker a place in the realm of architecture as a fine art.

Bars are certainly places to which we habitually return. Moreover, bars encourage an engagement quite apart from the narrative developed in conversation. The architectural narrative concerns the way we are accommodated in bars: how the place both fits a mood projected onto it, and simultaneously shapes a mood for those who gather there.

Susanne Langer captures this well when she distinguishes between an actual environment and a virtual 'environment'. The former is a part of the actual world as perceived. The latter occupies a virtual space, the space of the imagination. She writes,

> Architecture creates the semblance of that World which is the counterpart of a Self. It is a total environment made visible. Where the self is collective, as in a tribe, its World is communal; for personal Selfhood, it is the home. And as the actual environment of a being is a system of functional relations, so a virtual 'environment,' the created space of architecture, is a symbol of functional existence. This does not mean, however, that *signs* of important activities – hooks for implements, convenient benches, well-planned doors – play any part in its significance. In that false assumption lies the error of 'functionalism' – lies not very deep, but perhaps as deep as the theory itself goes. Symbolic expression is something miles removed from provident planning or good arrangement. It does not suggest things to do, but embodies the feeling, the rhythm, the passion or sobriety, frivolity or fear with which any things at all are done. That is the image of life that is created in buildings (...)
>
> (Langer 1994, 230)

Langer's 'symbolic expression' remains obscure. However, she recognizes both that aesthetic response to works of art involves a feeling (defiant of conceptual grasp) and also a symbol. (The making of a work of art involves communication, of some sort.)

Kant's exposition of aesthetic ideas will be of help to us here.

The utter beauty of bars, especially the ones mentioned in this book, is testimony to lives lived in bars. Graham's sharp observation that there is commonality between houses of worship and art museums is demonstrated by the fact that in each we come together to reflect upon our lives and our culture. We return to them to reassert our commitment and to *feel* ourselves at home. To the temple and the international art gallery I wish to add the bar.

Our experiences in these places extend beyond but most certainly include the built fabric of the building. In Adrian Gill's autobiographical *Pour Me*, he describes a basement bar, the Lindsey Club, a drinking den in Kensington run by two out-of-work (beyond work, to be brutally honest) ancient actresses, the bar now sadly gone,

> Downstairs there was a bald, half-size pool table on the tilt, an ancient jukebox that I only remember playing Sinatra crooning 'My Kind of Town', a short bar and a mismatched collection of tables and chairs. There were yellow lights with red shades like flung knickers and a carpet that had the texture of warm tar.
>
> The place was coated with nicotine and despair. It was the most hopelessly sad and loneliest room I've ever known.
>
> (Gill 2016, 9)

My own memory of that beautiful little place, sad as Gill pictures it, is of losing a sock. (How do you lose a sock? You look down at your feet and both shoes are tied properly but one of your socks is now missing. It remains, these forty-odd years, a mystery to me.)

There was another bar, Ward's Irish House, a dive beneath Piccadilly Circus: a disgrace in the eyes of the 'worthy'; those whom Nairn would bundle together, mockingly, as 'subtopia'.

My own memory of that bar is an image of a subterranean pit. This would have been nearly fifty years ago. I bought an album, *Adventures in Paradise*, by Minnie Riperton in the huge record shop fronting onto the Circus; and took it downstairs to Ward's, a cavernous Irish bar with a central island dimly lit in a yellowish 60-watt wash that petered out towards the peripheral areas, themselves a kind of unlit hinterland. These were furnished with bare wooden-top tables undergirded by cast ironwork and chairs too heavy to be picked up and chucked around. Back at the bar there was a drinker asleep with his head on the counter and a barman reading the racing form. No natural light penetrated the bar and so after a while it might have been three in the afternoon or three in the morning. (All very Edward Hopper.)

As the barman was ignoring me, I walked over to the telephone booth, which had a door that folded in half inwards as you opened it. Folding the door open, activated the 40-watt light bulb. (More yellow. More Hopper.) Opening the door illuminated the faded ochre wall across which were written, in 'near illegible purple' biro, a scattering of telephone numbers and obscenities. (All very Ed Kienholz.) I lifted the receiver and called a woman I had once been in love with and who had left me a year before and who looked a lot like Minnie Riperton. It rang and rang. After a while, I put the phone back in its cradle, unfolded the door, thereby turning off the light, and went back to the bar.

The barman slammed the flat of his hand hard upon the counter next to the head of the drinker and shouted, 'WAKE UP!' Obediently, the poor man opened his bleary eyes and tried to focus on the barman. After a slight delay he said, 'A pint of Guinness, please', and was duly served. Only then was I permitted to order my own pint, served with its thick creamy head, upon which the barman carved the figure of a shamrock. That entire image has remained with me these long years. Ward's of Piccadilly: now *that* was a bar. Hopper's paintings of people inhabiting architecture are popular – a woman in a diner late at night, an usherette in an auditorium – perhaps because they connect us to a feeling of isolation in a city.

The image of Ward's Irish House unites the visual character of the bar with a particular inner feeling. The image is at a point where the projection of the subject and the look of the bar connect. Architecture has this nature. The interior of the bar stands outwardly as a symbol of an inner feeling.

What this leaves us with is the dilemma identified and *felt* by Abel in Muñoz Molina's novel. His love for the Barcelona Pavilion seems challenged by his admiration for the watchman's shack by the side of the melon patch. The pavilion is a work of art. It is concocted from steel and glass and water and marble. There is the transparency that Vesely recognizes in the Paris café, where the distinction between interior and exterior is erased. There are no doors. There is a continuous passage from the water through to the sheltered space with its marble wall. The marble discloses the earth as that has been compacted over tens, perhaps hundreds of thousands of years, whereas the water with its fountain is constantly changing in form and matter. We are caught somewhere in the middle, with a rather measly lifespan. The building has its architectural references with its rejection of classicism in favour of modern composition. The light becomes a feature as does the air, each a sort of 'stuff'. It is a beautiful object of contemplation, and it specifies no particular use, if any at all. However, it is not a sculpture, since all its references connect it with architecture. It exhibits the medium specificity we have sought to clarify. The materials are used to make a functional building (yet with no specified function) and it carries within its form ideas about how materials over time can be seen to throw our lives into temporal perspective, whilst setting its face against the classical point of view.

On the other hand, Abel admires the craft of the built shack. This, I think, is the nearest Muñoz Molina gets to illustrating Scruton's argument about architecture *not* being a fine art. The Lindsey Club and Ward's are both particular places in which we find a certain kind of beauty, but it might be objected that such beauty is best accounted for by 'everyday aesthetics'. Nevertheless, they provide substantiation of a fit between a built environment and the state of mind of an occupant. Certainly, our response to such places, whether loved or loathed, is an aesthetic response.

'Interior Architecture', as it has come to be known, is the furnishing and decorative aspect of the interiors of buildings. It is partly legitimized by Kant, but also by Semper and Le Corbusier. Kant considered the cabinet maker a maker of architecture, as we have seen. Semper and the Navajo women weavers made vertical hangings which served as partitions and as narratives. Le Corbusier, in his address to CIAM II, 'The Minimal House', divided architecture into two separate tasks. The first was engineering, the second he calls 'biological'. The first of these tasks is to construct an exoskeleton of the 'minimal house'. The second is to have within that framework partitioned walls (non-load-bearing) which have the purpose of dividing the building into 'vessels','rooms' and 'spaces' (elsewhere termed 'membranes') and circulation:

> The dwelling place is a distinctly biological phenomenon.
>
> Yet the vessels, the rooms, the spaces which it implies are confined in an envelope of solid materials belonging to a static system.
>
> Biological event, static event; these are two distinct orders, two independent functions.
>
> (Corbusier and Jeanneret 1929)

These tasks are akin to Semper's woven partitions. For both men the sructures of the building with its columns (for Corbusier these are renamed 'pilotis' or 'stilts') are constructions that permit the interiors to be impermanently arranged as partitions. Thus, what for the classicists was a major feature of the design is relegated in Semper to a necessary adjunct to the building; something in the manner of a tent-pole. Corbusier calls the rooms of the house 'membranes' and these serve our biological and cultural needs.

> This is what we believe: As far as the '*minimum house*' (social tool that is indispensable to the present era) is concerned, architecture can center its attention on equipping the inside of the house. Depending on the problem (capacity), the size of the family, the sort of occupant (his way of life), the exposure to sun and winds, the topographical location (city planning), the architect of equipment can invent biological groupings within a static standard framework. Thus the industrial methods required here, as a result of the absolute transformation of existing elements, can be employed in any climate since they can be made to fit any and all local conditions.
>
> (Corbusier and Jeanneret 1929)

We could realize this distinction across the engineering/poetry divide introduced and discussed in Chapter 1.

However, it poses a problem for appreciating the interior of the Ward's Irish House as a work of architecture, since the beauty of that place is not designed within the medium of architecture. Its dilapidations do not bear the mark of an 'architectural intention'.

VI Optimism in architectural fiction

Perhaps, then, we should look for an example of a work of architecture that exhibits, on a small scale, something of the homeliness I find in small bars with the vision of great architecture. The Barcelona Pavilion is a contender, with its architectural ideals and its homely, domestic scale. However, a contemporary example is *House for Essex*, a collaborative venture designed by FAT's Charles Holland and Grayson Perry. It is a beautiful little jewel that might have been designed by Abel in another novel. It seems to fit both the desire Abel has for a clean modernity with his admiration for detail that comes from an artisan tradition. (Holland regularly posts on social media photographs he has taken of charming, eccentric architectural details. He has a very good eye for such gems.) *House for Essex* is a gorgeous little building, brimming with such detail. It comes to our rescue. For it neatly avoids either Arcadianism or Utopianism. It fictionalizes the life of a saint, and so avoids our difficulties with belief, myth and metaphysics. The narrative is presented as fiction and so we are able to entertain thoughts about her whilst not having to commit to her existence. Moreover, having fictionalized the saint we can see how the architecture and the interior design can be understood and how we can, thereby, engage in aesthetic experience under the rubric of architecture as an art-kind.

Moreover, it is a shrine to a fictional woman,

> The building sits at the end of the lane like a rural chapel in the middle of a green meadow. 'It should just settle into the place and not change it,' said Holland.
>
> The design is centred around the fictional character Julie Cope, conceived by Perry as an 'Essex Everywoman' (...)
>
> Iconography depicts Julie as a saint – from mouldings on the glossy green tiling and an aluminium weather vein on the outside of the house to tapestries and ceramic statues inside.
>
> Behind a set of bright red double doors, an entrance hall with primary coloured paintwork leads to a kitchen with a herringbone parquet floor, followed by a chapel-like space with a tall pitched ceiling and rows of arched windows set high into the walls.

FIGURE 9.4 *Charles Holland (FAT Architecture) and Grayson Perry, House for Essex, 2015, photograph © Jack Hobhouse.*

Two large tapestries depicting Julie's life, from her birth to her divorce and eventually her death, hang from the walls.

> A motorbike hoisted up to the ceiling of the chapel represents a collision with a curry delivery driver, with which Julie met her end – a tombstone in the front garden marks her final resting place at 61.
>
> (Mairs 2015)

Here we have the institution of mythology, recognized as fiction. Our imaginations are required to experience the 'chapel' as a shrine for the dead woman who at once represents Essex and to *see* the quotidian imbued with fictional sanctity.

The building is part of a series commissioned by Alain de Botton's *Living Architecture*. The domestic spaces are part of a drive by *Living Architecture* to expand the discussion of contemporary architecture. Each of the buildings is an example of architecture conceived as a fine art.

The tapestries illustrating the life of the fictional saint provide the counterpart to Semper's partitions and the Navajo women's weaving of narrative. The motorbike, hoisted into the air in the interior, is reminiscent of bars that hang all manner of equipment from their ceilings, often but not always, around a theme. However, in *House for Essex*, the bike becomes part of the narrative. It is thought through, and that makes its intention the intention of an architect (or, in this case the architect and artist collaboration).

VII Afterword

It is now established, I believe, that architecture is a fine art; but that, also, most buildings are not works of architecture.

REFERENCES

Alberti, L. B., (1988) *On the Art of Building in Ten Books*, (trans.) Joseph Rykwert, Neil Leach, Robert Tavenor, Cambridge, MA: MIT Press

Aristotle (1984a) *The Complete Works of Aristotle*, vol. 1, (The Revised Oxford Translation) (ed.) Jonathan Barnes, Princeton: Princeton University Press

Aristotle (1984b) *The Complete Works of Aristotle*, vol. 2, (The Revised Oxford Translation) (ed.) Jonathan Barnes, Princeton: Princeton University Press

Auden, W. H., (2011) *The Age of Anxiety: A Baroque Eclogue*, edited with an Introduction by Alan Jacobs, Oxford: Princeton University Press

Bakewell, S., (2016) *At the Existentialist Café: Freedom, Being and Apricot Cocktails*, London: Chatto & Windus

Baudelaire, C., (2021) *Paris Spleen*, (trans.) Martin Sorrell, London: Alma Classics

Beauvoir, S. de., (1992) *Letters to Sartre*, London: Vintage

Beauvoir, S. de., (2000) *America Day by Day*, California: University of California Press

Blackburn, S., (1998) *Ruling Passions*, Oxford: Clarendon Press

Bustin, J., (2014) *Tablet II*, mixed media, can be seen in colour online. It was accessed on 28 March at: https://www.inglebygallery.com/exhibitions/5490/works/01b7cb48750f15/

Callan, E., (1965) 'Allegory in *The Age of Anxiety*' in *Twentieth Century Literature*, vol. 10, no. 4, pp. 155–165. January 1965

Casati, R., and Varzi, A., (1999) *Parts and Places*, MIT

Colquhoun, A., (2002) *Modern Architecture*, Oxford History of Art, OUP

Complete Cocktails (2013) Accessed online on 31 August at: http://www.completecocktails.com/DrinksByName/C.aspx?Page=40

Coquinaria (2019) Medieval Blacmange Recipe, accessed on 15 October 2021 at: https://coquinaria.nl/en/medieval-blancmange/

Corbusier and Jeanneret, P., (1929) The International Congress for Modern Architecture [CIAM] 2nd Congress at Frankfurt-am-Main – September, 1929 'ANALYSIS OF THE FUNDAMENTAL ELEMENTS OF THE PROBLEM OF "THE MINIMUM HOUSE"' accessed on 30 August 2022 at: https://modernistarchitecture.wordpress.

com/2011/09/14/le-corbusier%E2%80%99s-%E2%80%9Cciam-2-1929%E2%80%9D-1929/

Critchley, S., (2009) *The Guardian*, online, accessed on 25 June 2021 at: https://www.theguardian.com/commentisfree/belief/2009/jun/22/heidegger-religion-philosophy

Duchamp, M., (1975) 'Apropos of "Readymades"', in *The Essential Writings of Duchamp*, (eds.) Michel Sanouillet and Elmer Peterson, London and New York: Thames and Hudson

Eisenman, P., (1996) 'Post-functionalism', in *Theorizing a New Agenda for Architecture*, (ed.) Kate Nesbitt, Princeton Architectural Press

Eliot, T. S., (1998) 'Tradition and the Individual Talent' in *The Sacred Wood and Major Early Essays*, Mineola, New York: Dover Publications

Evans, R., (1997) 'Translations from Drawing to Building', in his, *Translations from Drawing to Building and Other Essays*, London: Architectural Association Publications, 1997

Extremely Large Telescope, (2022) Wikipedia page, accessed on 28 January 2022 at: https://en.wikipedia.org/wiki/Extremely_Large_Telescope

Forty, A., (2004) *Words and Buildings: A Vocabulary of Modern Architecture*, London and New York: Thames and Hudson

Gill, A. A., (2016) *Pour Me: A Life*, London: Weidenfield & Nicolson

Graham, G., (2007) *The Re-enchantment of the World: Art versus Religion*, Oxford: Oxford University Press

Greenberg, C., (1995) 'Modernist Painting' in *The Philosophy of Art: Readings Ancient and Modern*, (eds.) Alex Neill and Aaron Ridley, London: McGraw-Hill

Greene, D., (1999) 'L.A.W.U.N. Project Number One: Bottery', in *Concerning Archigram,* (ed.) Dennis Crompton, London: Archigram Archives

Greene, D., Goodbun, J., and Cunningham, D., (2001) 'Architecture and the Rain', in *The Journal of Architecture,* vol. 6, pp. 195–200

Guyer, P., (2021) *A Philosopher Looks at Architecture*, Cambridge: Cambridge University Press

Harries, K., (1997) *The Ethical Function of Architecture*, Cambridge, MA: MIT

Harries, K., Scruton, R., and Illies, C., (2017) 'Building Thinking Asking: What Is the Right Way to Do Philosophy of Architecture,' in *Architecture Philosophy*, vol. 3, no. 1. pp. 9–24

Harwood, E., (2021) *The Guardian*, Obituaries, 'Trevor Dannatt'harwood, Saturday 20 February 2021

Heaney, S., (2018) 'The Conway Stewart', in his *100 Poems*, London: Faber & Faber

Heidegger, M., (2013) *Poetry, Language, Thought*, (trans.) Albert Hofstadter, New York: Harper and Row

Hume, D., (1978) *A Treatise of Human Nature*, Oxford: Clarendon

Hume, D., (1985) 'Of the Standard of Taste' in his, *Essays Moral, Political and Literary*, (ed.) E. Miller, Indianapolis: Literary Classics

Jacobs, A., (2011) 'Introduction' in *The Age of Anxiety: A Baroque Eclogue*, Auden, W. H., op. cit, Oxford: Princeton University Press

Jung, C., (2019) *Memories, Dreams, Reflections: An Autobiography*, London: William Collins

Kant, I., (1964) *Critique of Pure Reason*, (trans.) Norman Kemp Smith, London: Macmillan & Co

Kant, I., (1987) *Critique of Judgment*, (trans.) Walter H. Pluhar, Indianapolis: Hackett

Kant, I., (2004) *Prolegomena to Any Future Metaphysics*, (ed.) Gary Hatfield, Cambridge: Cambridge University Press

Keith, L., (2020) 'Hegra, an Ancient City in Saudi Arabia Untouched for Millennia, Makes Its Public Debut', *Smithsonian Magazine*, Travel, 23 November, accessed on 3 April 2022 at: https://www.smithsonianmag.com/travel/hegra-ancient-city-saudi-arabia-untouched-for-millennia-makes-its-public-debut-180976361/

Klein, S., (2020) *The See through House: My Father in Full Colour*, London: Chatto and Windus

Kristeller, P. O., (1951) 'The Modern System of the Arts: A Study in the History of Aesthetics (I)', in *Journal of the History of Ideas*, vol. 12, no. 4, pp. 496–527 October

Kristeller, P. O., (1952) 'The Modern System of the Arts: A Study in the History of Aesthetics (II)', in *Journal of the History of Ideas*, vol. 13, no. 1, pp. 17–46 January, 1952

Kruft, H.-W., (1994) *A History of Architectural Theory from Vitruvius to the Present*, New York: Princeton Architectural Press

Langer, S., (1994) 'Feeling and Form', in *Art and Its Significance*, (ed.) Stephen David Ross, New York: SUNY

Lemoine, B., (2019) Tour.Eiffel website, accessed on 2 October 2020 at: https://www.toureiffel.paris/en/news/130-years/artists-who-protested-eiffel-tower

Lopes, D. Mc., (2014) *Beyond Art*, Oxford: Oxford University Press

Mairs, J., (2015) 'Grayson Perry and FAT Reveal the Elaborate Interiors of Their House for Essex', in *Dezeen*, accessed on 31 August 2022 at: https://www.dezeen.com/2015/05/15/house-for-essex-fat-grayson-perry-charles-holland-living-architecture-alain-de-botton/

Mallgrave, H. F., (1989) 'Introduction', in Semper, G., *The Four Elements of Architecture, and Other Writings*, (trans.) Harry Francis Mulgrave and Wolfgang Herrmann, Cambridge: Cambridge University Press

Maupassant, G. de., (2017) in Yves Bonnefoy, *Poetry and Photography*, London, New York, Calcutta: Seagull Books

Muñoz Molina, A., (2009) 'Un edificio, un símbolo', in *El Pais*, 16 January, accessed on 20 May 2021 at: https://elpais.com/diario/2009/01/17/babelia/1232152754_850215.html
Muñoz Molina, A., (2015) *In the Night of Time*, London: Serpent's Tail
Nairn, I., (2017) *Nairn's Paris*, London: Notting Hill Editions
Olsen, S. L., (2020) *Arabian Rock Art Heritage*, accessed on 3 April 2022 at: http://saudi-archaeology.com/sites/madain-saleh/
Ousterhout, R., (1984) 'Meaning and Architecture: A Medieval View', *Reflections*, vol. 2, no. 1, pp. 34–46
Pallasmaa, J., (2012) 'Spaces of Memory and Imagination', in *The Eyes of the Skin*, Chichester: John Wiley & Sons
Parsons, G., (2016) *The Philosophy of Design*, Cambridge: Polity Press
Plato (1927) *Phædrus*, in *Five Dialogues of Plato Bearing on Poetic Inspiration*, (trans.) J. Wright, London and Toronto: J. M. Dent
Porphyrios, D., (1996) 'The Relevance of Classical Architecture' in *Theorizing a New Agenda for Architecture: An Anthology of Architectural Theory 1965–1995*, (ed.) Kate Nesbitt, New York: Princeton Architecture Press
Rowe, C., (1998) 'Introduction to Five Architects', in *Architecture|Theory|since 1968* (ed.) E. Miachel Hays, A Columbia Book of Architecture
St John Wilson, C., (1992) *Architectural Reflections: Studies in the Philosophy and Practice of Architecture*, Oxford: Butterworth Architecture
Samuels, A., (1986) *Jung and the Post-Jungians*, London and New York: Routledge
Sartre, J-P., (2004) *The Imaginary*, (trans.) Jonathan Weber, Oxford: Routledge
Sartre, J-P., (2017) 'Paris under the Occupation,' in his, *The Aftermath of War* (trans.) Chris Turner, London, New York, Calcutta: Seagull Books. (The story appears as the 'Appendix'.)
Scruton, R., (1974) *Art and Imagination*, London: Methuen
Scruton, R., (1996) 'Why Lampposts and Phone Booths Matter,' in *City Journal*. Published online and accessed on 3 October 2020 at: https://www.city-journal.org/html/why-lampposts-and-phone-booths-matter-12001.html
Scruton, R., (2002) *The Aesthetics of Architecture*, New York: Princeton University Press
Scruton, R., (2005) *Gentle Regrets*, London: Continuum
Scruton, R., (2006) *Sexual Desire*, London: Continuum
Scruton, R., (2009) 'Everyday Beauty', in his, *Beauty*, Oxford: OUP
Scruton, R., (2012) 'A Guarded Response', in *Scruton's Aesthetics*, (eds.) Andy Hamilton and Nick Zangwill, London: Palgrave Macmillan

Scruton, R., (2014) *The Soul of the World*, Princeton and Oxford: Princeton University Press

Semper, G., (1989) *The Four Elements of Architecture, and Other Writings*, (trans.) Harry Francis Mulgrave and Wolfgang Herrmann, Cambridge: Cambridge University Press

Sen, A., (2021) *At Home in the World*, London: Allen Layne

Sörböm (2002), 'The Classical Concept of Mimesis', in *A Companion to Art Theory*, (eds.) Paul Smith and Carolyn Wilde, Oxford: Blackwell

Steinbeck, J., (1987) 'Stalingrad, 1949,' in *The Faber Book of Reportage*, London: Faber and Faber

Storr, A., (1998) *The Essential Jung: Selected Writings*, London: Fontana

Thanhauser, S., (2022), *Worn: A People's History of Clothing*, London: Allen Lane

Tremlett, G., (2018) 'Gerda Taro: "deathbed photo" of One of World's First War Photographers Found', in the *Guardian*, accessed on 21 April 2022 at: https://www.theguardian.com/world/2018/jan/19/deathbed-photo-of-war-photographer-gerda-taro-discovered

van Eck, C., (1999) 'Enduring Principles of Architecture in Alberti's *On the Art of Building*: How Did Alberti Set Out to Formulate Them?' in *The Journal of Architecture*, vol. 4, no. 2, pp. 119–27 Summer

Vesely, D., (2006) *Architecture in the Age of Divided Representation*, MIT Press

Waxman, L., (2017) *Keep Walking Intently: The Ambulatory Art of the Surrealists, the Situationist International, and Fluxus*, Berlin: Sternberg Press

Wikipedia (2021) 'Palaver (Custom)' accessed on 31 February 2022 at: https://en.wikipedia.org/wiki/Palaver_(custom)

Winters, E., (2007) *Aesthetics and Architecture*, London and New York: Continuum

Wittgenstein, L., (2007) *Remarks on Colour*, California: California University Press

Wollheim, R., (1973) 'The Work of Art as Object', in his, *On Art and the Mind*, London: Allen Lane

Wollheim, R., (1980) 'Are the Criteria for Works of Art Aesthetically Relevant?' in his, *Art and Its Objects*, (2nd edition), Cambridge: CUP

Wollheim, R., (1984) *The Thread of Life*, New Haven and London: Yale University Press

Wollheim, R., (1987) *Painting as an Art*, London and New York: Thames and Hudson

Wollheim, R., (1993) *The Mind and Its Depths*, Cambridge, MA: Harvard University Press

Wollheim, R., (2012) 'Danto's Gallery of Indiscernibles' in *Danto and His Critics* (ed.) Mark Rollins, (2nd edition), Chichester: John Wiley & Sons

INDEX

www.ingramcontent.com/pod-product-compliance
Lightning Source LLC
Chambersburg PA
CBHW071839230426
43671CB00012B/2001
* 9 7 8 1 3 5 0 2 1 1 0 0 1 *